Praise for

Worthy of a Miracle

"Linda's story is an amazing example of God's mighty power and faithfulness. If you're believing God for something that seems impossible, let this book empower you to believe you are worthy and that he is with you!"

—**Lysa TerKeurst,** *New York Times* bestselling author and president of Proverbs 31 Ministries

"Linda Kuhar extends an invitation to find an extraordinary God at work in the middle of our ordinary lives. She offers faith, encouragement, and, most of all, hope. Whether you're going through a difficult time or are simply looking for inspiration and a new perspective, *Worthy of a Miracle* will meet you where you are and help you see what could be."

—**Holley Gerth,** *Wall Street Journal* bestselling author of *You're Already Amazing*

"I knew Linda's story would be inspiring, but I had no idea how much her book would touch my heart as a woman, a wife, a parent, and a believer. Seeing how God orchestrated small and life-changing miracles in her life literally moved me to tears as I witnessed the tangible proof of the power of God at work. Her story is a beautiful reminder of God's sovereignty, packed with scriptural promises and practical steps for growing our relationship with God, while reminding us all that we are worthy of his miracles too."

—**Tracie Miles,** Christian speaker and writer, and author of two best-selling books, *Your Life Still Counts* and *Stressed-Less Living*

"My friend Linda is what I call 'Gospel-strong!' In the pages of *Worthy of a Miracle,* you will see how in Linda's weakness, Jesus made her Gospel-strong! You will not regret buying this book; you'll like it so much, you will buy five more for your family and friends."

—**Derwin L. Gray,** lead pastor at Transformation Church, author of *Crazy Grace for Crazy Times* Bible Study (Lifeway)

"I heard Linda's cancer story numerous times through our connection with the Team In Training program with Leukemia and Lymphoma Society, but reading her book gave me a brand new perspective on the challenges, fears, choices, and triumphs she, her family, and her friends faced in her fight against lymphoma. As her coach for her first half marathon, just six months after her coma, I never saw her back down on her commitment to train for and complete her 13.1-mile victory, even when the going got tough. What I did see was how that commitment inspired her fellow teammates to persevere. I admire that she has the courage to build on what she learned from that experience to go after her purpose in life."

—**Beth Carty,** Team In Training coach for the Leukemia and Lymphoma Society

"Linda's book is her personal, beautiful, and inspiring story of God's faithfulness. Her story is for any woman who has ever felt she was not worthy of a miracle. Linda learned how to open her heart to receive the Lord's gift of amazing love as God 'used a physical coma to fully reveal to her how to have a relationship with Jesus.'"

—**Janice LaVore-Fletcher,** PCC, MCC, BCC, president of Christian Coach Institute, LLC

Worthy of
a Miracle

Love & Live Jesus! ♡

Linda Kuhar

Worthy of a Miracle

5 SIMPLE TRUTHS *for* BELIEVING *and* RECEIVING GOD'S LOVE

Linda Kuhar

LEAFWOOD
PUBLISHERS
an imprint of Abilene Christian University Press

WORTHY OF A MIRACLE
5 Simple Truths for Believing and Receiving God's Love

L E A F W O O D
P U B L I S H E R S
an imprint of Abilene Christian University Press

Copyright © 2015 by Linda Kuhar

978-0-89112-465-8
Printed in the United States of America

Scripture quotations, unless otherwise noted, are from The Holy Bible, New International Version®, NIV®. Copyright © 1973, 1978, 1984, 2011 by Biblica, Inc.® Used by permission. All rights reserved worldwide.

Scripture quotations noted NLT are taken from the New Living Translation, Copyright ©1996, 2004, 2007 by Tyndale House Foundation. Used by permission of Tyndale House Publishers, Inc., Carol Stream, IL 60188. All rights reserved.

Scripture quotations noted NASB are taken from the New American Standard Bible® Copyright © 1960, 1962, 1963, 1968, 1971, 1972, 1973, 1975, 1977, 1995 by The Lockman Foundation. Used by permission.

Scripture quotations noted *The Message* taken from *The Message*. Copyright 1993, 1994, 1995, 1996, 2000, 2001, 2002. Used by permission of NavPress Publishing Group.

The author is represented by and this book is published in association with the literary agency of WordServe Literary Group, Ltd., www.wordserveliterary.com.

Library of Congress Cataloging-in-Publication Data
Kuhar, Linda, 1974-
  Worthy of a miracle : 5 simple truths for believing & receiving God's love / Linda Kuhar.
    pages cm
  ISBN 978-0-89112-465-8
  1. God (Christianity)--Love. 2. Self-esteem--Religious aspects--Christianity. 3. Faith. I. Title.
  BT140.K84 2015
  277.3'083092--dc23
  [B]
                                                                        2015017907

Cover design by Thinkpen Design, LLC
Interior text design by Sandy Armstrong, Strong Design

Leafwood Publishers is an imprint of Abilene Christian University Press
ACU Box 29138
Abilene, Texas 79699

1-877-816-4455
www.leafwoodpublishers.com

15 16 17 18 19 20 / 7 6 5 4 3 2 1

This book is dedicated to you, dear reader.

While I don't know your faith journey, I do know everyone

struggles, at times, simply to believe.

My prayer for you is that, through connecting with my story,

your faith will be refreshed and strengthened.

You *are* worthy of a miracle!

Acknowledgments

To my Lord and Savior, Jesus Christ: You created me to be your beautiful beloved daughter. No matter how many times I fall, you so graciously love me right where I am. You love every part of me. I am worthy because of you. I cannot imagine how glorious it will be to meet you face to face. Thank you for the gift of life and your precious Holy Spirit living inside of me. I love you with every fiber of my being.

To my husband, Todd: You are the hero in my life story. You never give up on me. You believe in the impossible and therefore it is possible. Thank you for not letting me quit. It's an honor to be your wife and run the race of life with you until the very end. I love you forever.

To my daughter, Megan: You are my heart with legs. Your wise, courageous, creative spirit inspires me daily. I love you to the moon and back times infinity. Thank you for teaching me to laugh! Being your mom will *always* be my favorite thing on earth.

To my mom: I will never know what it was like to sit beside my hospital bed countless hours monitoring machines to keep me alive. Your prayers, your tears, and your heart are why I am here today. Thank you, Momma. I love you always.

To my family: I love every one of you with my whole heart. Thank you for your unconditional love and support my entire life.

To my friends: So many . . . who pour out so much love and encouragement. Thank you for believing in me and accepting me with all my imperfections. My life is full because of you. I treasure you.

To my book coaches and sisters in Christ: Lee McCracken, encourager and award-winning author of *A Prayer and a Pink Pedicure*, and Peg Robarchek, book editor and award-winning author and poet. Because of your brilliance, compassion, and unfailing belief, *Worthy of a Miracle* was born. I will never stop thanking both of you.

To my medical team: Your dedication to your patients' health and healing impacts the world with every breath we take. Thank you will *never* be enough for what you do.

To the Leukemia and Lymphoma Society and Team In Training participants: You are making a difference. Thank you for every step you have taken and continue to take to cure blood cancer. I love you. Go Team!

To my church: I am spiritually fit because you challenge me daily to honor God with my whole life. Thank you for stretching me.

To the Christian Life Coach community: Together we are making a difference in the kingdom. It's a privilege to serve with you.

To my agent and publisher: Thank you for taking a chance on me and making my dream come true.

Contents

PART TWO

Part One

CHAPTER ONE

Unworthy

MAYBE YOU'VE NEVER FELT UNWORTHY. Maybe you've never thought, *If I were prettier, maybe the people I love would love me more.* (Go ahead and substitute "slimmer" or "blonder" or "taller" or "more athletic" or whatever your version of "not-cover-model material" might be.)

Or maybe your not-good-enough mantra sounds like one of these: If I were smarter, maybe I wouldn't have to work so hard. If I were more talented, maybe I'd make more money and have a job I love. If I were a better mother, maybe my kids would be better behaved, make better grades, have more friends. If I were a better wife, maybe my husband would love me unconditionally and my marriage would be as picture-perfect as the couple next door and the people one pew ahead of us at church on Sunday.

Or maybe this, *If I were a better person, maybe God would answer my prayer . . . ease my suffering . . . heal me.*

Does any of that sound familiar?

If you've never felt unworthy, I'll admit it right here—I'm just a little bit envious. A sense of unworthiness is an invisible badge I wore most of my life. Unworthy of love, unworthy of success, unworthy of the good life, unworthy, even, of God's love. Ultimately even unworthy of the miracles all my friends and family witnessed God working in my life. Everybody, it seemed, was able to see those miracles except me. What if the same thing is true for you? What if everybody in your life can see just how worthy you are and just how miraculously God is affirming that? What if you are the only one who is blind to the truth?

∽ ∽ ∽

I've worn that invisible badge of unworthiness since I was a little girl. But the first time I fully realized how unworthy I felt was the day I graduated from college in June 1997. Clearly, I should have been celebrating my accomplishments—that I had overcome some major obstacles, including others' predictions that I would never succeed.

Like so many other times in my life, however, I saw not the miracle, but what I perceived as a truth no one else could see—that I did not deserve the diploma or the applause or the congratulations.

My entire family had turned out for the big event, including my in-laws. I had married my high school sweetheart, Todd, at the young age of nineteen. Over the years, my mother-in-law, Judy, had become my number one fan, best friend, and supporter. My teen years had been filled with drama and rebellion (if you consider getting arrested for shoplifting a little wild—and I certainly would if it were my daughter!). During those troublesome times, Judy accepted and loved me unconditionally—something not every woman would be capable of if the son she loved brought home a girlfriend who had the kind of problems I did.

I had never been a great student in school. Failing English in seventh grade and getting kicked off the cheerleading team before the season even began confirmed to me that I was a loser, and not just when it came to schoolwork. In eleventh grade, my high school guidance counselor told me I would not be able to go to college because of my poor grades. Don't count on having any type of career, she told me.

For some reason—some might call it a miracle—I took that judgment and turned it into the motivation, during my senior year, to make the A-B honor roll for the first time in my life. That success gave me the confidence to attend college and study hard.

And along the way, Judy Kuhar believed in me—more than the guidance counselor, maybe more than some people in my own family, and certainly more than I believed in myself. Her belief carried me through those long nights of study when I was a young newlywed preparing for exams.

Because of my history, college graduation was an emotional day for me. I was accomplishing more than I ever thought possible. There was even a chance that I would be graduating with honors, something I would not know for sure until just before the graduation ceremony. As students lined up, college officials handed out special gold tassels for honor students. My family would not know whether or not I had accomplished my almost unimaginable goal until they saw me walking down the aisle and they saw what tassel I was wearing.

To my shock, just as I was lining up for the ceremony, my biological father, his wife, and my two half-sisters arrived. I had seen my father only a few times since I was three years old. I could count on one hand the number of times I had seen him since then.

Tears welled up in my eyes. *Why would he be here for me today? Why would he want to see me?*

My heart raced and a lump rose in my throat. After all the years he had barely made an effort to see or talk to me, I found it hard to believe he cared about my achievements. He did seem proud of me, but instead of feeling happy about his presence, all I could think was, *Linda, you do not deserve this, all these people here to see you. Graduating from college is really not that big a deal. People do it all the time.*

I tried to ignore the belittling voice, but feelings of unworthiness saturated me.

Suddenly, my graduation gown felt heavy, as if it could swallow me whole. I did not feel good enough about myself to believe I deserved all that was happening that day—the accomplishments, the recognition, the attention, and especially the love.

After acknowledging my father and receiving his hug, I headed to the back of the auditorium to line up for the ceremony. As I did so, one of my professors called out, "Linda Kuhar, congratulations! Here is your tassel. You are graduating with honors."

I stared at the gold tassel he held out to me. I could not absorb all that was happening.

All I could do was respond, "Really, there's no way I am an honor student."

Marching down the aisle to the graduation music, I looked out of the corner of my eye to see my mother-in-law's face. She was grinning from ear to ear, about to burst. She mouthed to me, "I knew you did it, baby! I knew it!"

I swallowed hard to keep the tears back. I was unable to allow myself to believe I was worthy of this accomplishment.

∾ ∾ ∾

In my work as a Christian life coach, I've seen this deep sense of unworthiness more times than I can count.

I have talked with people who do their best to follow Christ, people who give of themselves to others, people who are pillars of their church and rocks for their friends and family—yet they still feel unworthy. No matter how much they pray, no matter how many mission trips they've made, no matter how much Scripture they can quote, in some dark corner of their hearts, they feel unworthy. No matter how much good they try to do in the name of the Lord, they are *positive* they come up short in the eyes of the Lord.

When I was in my midtwenties, I became close friends with a woman who lived nearby. She and I both had toddlers, and we both loved Jesus. Amanda was a beautiful young lady and an incredible wife and mother. When we first met, she might have been a few pounds overweight. But who doesn't have extra weight to lose after having a baby, right?

Over the years of our friendship, Amanda didn't lose that baby weight. She gained more. She eventually gained a tremendous amount of weight.

Watching her struggle, constantly trying diet after diet and losing her self-confidence instead of weight, broke my heart. None of her weight-loss strategies seemed to work for any length of time.

Only when Amanda faced her feelings of unworthiness did she permanently lose the weight—without surgery or a fad diet.

The bottom line was that my beautiful friend had stuffed herself with food for years trying to bury the guilt and shame she carried from the abortion she had when she was a teenager. But now she was free and living a healthy life after discovering her worth as God's beloved daughter—and by accepting the forgiveness God offers so freely.

A sense of unworthiness weighs especially heavily, I think, on women.

We begin the search for worthiness as little girls. We learn very young to build our lives—and our worth—on unattainable fairy tales. We learn to fantasize endlessly about our future soul mate and dream of our wedding day. We plan to live happily ever after with a husband—the perfect Prince Charming—who will complete us and our lives. Worthiness is attached to this fairy tale at a very young age. Worthiness is equated with having the right people accept and approve of who we are as human beings. As long as "they" say we are enough, then we must be worthy.

This detrimental thought becomes etched in our mind. It will set us up for a life of always coming up short—because *when we don't live the fairy tale, it must surely be because we are unworthy.*

In today's culture, it doesn't stop with the age-old fairy tale, either. Adding fuel to the fire is social media. Think about everything you see on Facebook, on Pinterest, all over the Internet—everything we see entices us to believe that if we are anything less than picture perfect then we are nothing. Scrolling through our phones hour after hour, comparing ourselves to everyone else, leaves us feeling not good enough.

Unworthiness hardens into a core belief of who we are.

I am here to tell you one thing: that sense of unworthiness is a lie.

You are a child of God. That's how worthy you are.

You and I have inherited birthright status through Jesus. This means we have rights, privileges, possessions, and authority as soon as we accept Jesus as our Savior. Romans 8:17 tells us the real truth: "Now if we are children, then we are heirs—heirs of God and co-heirs with Christ."

How would you feel if your child told you they did not feel worthy to be your son or daughter? That they did not deserve to have your last name? It would break my heart. But no matter how unworthy my daughter might feel, the fact would continue to be that she would still possess my last name. No matter what my daughter might think or do, I would continue to love her more deeply every single day. I'm proud of her when she's confident and strong—and when she's weak, scared, uncertain, and even rebellious, I want nothing more in the world than to wrap my arms around her and remind her how much she is loved and that she will always be my precious girl. And I'm betting that if you have children, you feel the same.

Can you possibly imagine how much more we are loved, adored, and cherished by our heavenly Father, the One who created us? And how much compassion he has for us?

The Bible tells us we are his children. "See how very much our Father loves us, for he calls us his children, and that is what we are!" (1 John 3:1 NLT).

You were created by God, and it is time to reject the lie that you are anything other than his child.

∾ ∾ ∾

Rejecting the lie is easier said than done, isn't it?

That's why I wrote this book—to offer my own experiences in learning to reject that lie and to pick up the real truth, the whole truth, and nothing but the most empowering truth—God created you and you are worthy of his love and care!

Worthy of a Miracle is the story of my own journey from this self-defeating belief in my own unworthiness to my current state of asking for God's grace to believe I am worthy of his love. It is the story of my miraculous healing and rescue from the brink of death. It is the story of the years I spent hiding how I truly felt about the miracles everyone except me could believe.

Worthy of a Miracle is also a guidebook for any woman who wants to more fully own her inheritance as a daughter of God. And it is for you, no matter where you currently are on that journey. This is not a step-by-step instruction manual on how to *become* "worthy," but rather an inspirational practice to deepen your awareness of how worthy you already are by accepting the relationship Jesus offers. By sharing my story, I hope you'll find help for your own journey to fully embrace the truth that you are a child of God and, therefore, worthy of his love, his care, his protection, his grace, his mercy—every good gift, in fact.

This is the core of my message to you: *You are a child of God and, therefore, worthy of his love, his care, his protection, his grace, and his mercy.*

To walk you through your own shift in perspective about how worthy you are, I'll share with you the most important lesson I've learned along the way: Jesus is the answer.

That's right. Jesus is the answer. We all know that, don't we? Nothing revolutionary there.

But how do we really live that truth?

We may know that Jesus is the answer in making good decisions for our families, in our careers, in choosing our spouses, in all the big decisions that shape our lives. However, Jesus is also the answer in how we live our lives and interact with others daily. And even more important, Jesus is the answer to engaging with ourselves, especially with our thoughts and attitudes about who we are as people—as beautifully unique individuals truly worthy of love.

Over the years of my own healing, I've learned how to use an acronym as a simple reminder of how to live in the truth about my relationship with God. Here's what it looks like:

- Just live today.
- Expect miracles.
- Speak truth.
- Use your gifts.
- Start now!

We'll explore each one of these ideas more thoroughly later in the book. We'll talk about how I try to do these things not just in my actions but in my thoughts and attitudes. We'll talk about how you can use these concepts to change your life, too, and come to live each day believing a little more that you are worthy of God's love, protection, and grace.

Please notice I haven't said that I live in a state of knowing every day, deep in my soul, that I'm worthy of God's love. I wish I could claim that. On some days I still look at my weakness, my imperfections, my shaky faith, and wonder if maybe I'm the only person in the world whom God doesn't really love unconditionally. No matter how many times God shows up with miracles big and small, no matter how many times I experience God's grace, I still have those days when I wake up and am tempted to go back to believing I am unworthy.

I can tell you that, while writing this book, I have spent days and even weeks doubting that I was worthy to share my story and my message with you. At times I would get paralyzed with insecurity and tell my husband and my editors and my friends that I was going to quit writing the book, that it was just too much for me. I was not good enough.

In fact, at times, it seems like a miracle that I ever finished this book.

Part of the miracle, for all of us, is that God keeps showing up for us, even when we doubt. We don't have to be perfect in our faith or in our lives. We just have to keep watching for the ways God shows up every day.

And God does show up. That's how worthy we are.

My prayer for you, dear reader, is that you will find courage within these pages to seek Jesus just as you are and receive his love today. No performance is necessary—just be yourself.

That may seem like a miracle. But if no one else has told you today, let me. You, too, are worthy of a miracle!

CHAPTER TWO

Changed

"YOU HAVE A TEN-CENTIMETER MASS behind your heart."

Those are the words that would change the course of my life . . . forever.

I can recall every hour, every minute of May 11, 2009. It started right where I'm sitting now as I type these words.

It was the Monday after Mother's Day. My husband and daughter had left, him for work and her for school. It was around eight o'clock, and I was quite cozy, snuggled in my favorite living room chair. We lived in a lovely suburban neighborhood in south Charlotte, North Carolina—the hometown of Billy Graham and a community often called the City of Churches. With a nice, warm cup of coffee in my hand, I was reading my favorite devotional book, *Jesus Calling*.

My long blond hair was tied up in a ponytail because I did not feel like washing it that day. I'd been a tad under the weather for the last few days, fighting a persistent cough. I had tucked tissues in the pocket of my robe just in case I needed them. Looking out the living room window, I saw that the overcast sky promised one of those dreary late-spring days that seemed to give me permission to stay inside.

I was glad, because I didn't have much energy anyway. A dreary day was a good excuse to go back to bed.

My sense of feeling dragged down wasn't all physical, either. I felt sad. It had been almost two years since my mother-in-law, Judy, lost her fight against cancer. My daughter, Megan, was seven years old when her Grammy died, and I still found myself wondering if she would remember all those sweet tea parties, the times when she played with Grammy's dolls and dressed up in Grammy's jewelry from head to toe. My heart still felt broken that my little girl, now nine, would grow up without her grandmother, without this amazingly loving woman who had made such a positive difference in my own young life.

Reminiscing about Judy and how much I missed her brought tears to my eyes.

With the tears came that nagging cough again. I couldn't seem to clear my throat. And then came one hard cough into my tissue. When I pulled the tissue away from my face, I noticed something odd—a tiny spot of blood.

"Great, now I suppose I'll have to go to the doctor," I mumbled under my breath.

Mostly aggravated, but also a little nervous, I called my doctor's office to set up an appointment sometime over the next few days. As the receptionist looked through appointment times, I mentioned the blood, almost an afterthought. To my surprise, when I mentioned the blood, she asked me to come in immediately.

Driving over to the doctor's office, I realized how exhausted I really was.

This will work out perfectly, I thought. *I can get a prescription and then go back home and sleep until it's time to pick up Meg from school. I just need to sleep it off and I'll feel like myself again.*

The doctor appeared a little concerned as he listened to my lungs. I'd known Dr. Bauer for a while and felt confident under his care. He's a handsome gentleman. But I did not find the frown on his face too attractive that morning.

"I hear some wheezing," he said. "I suspect you have bronchitis. But why don't we get a chest X-ray just to rule out pneumonia."

He turned back to his file and scribbled on his prescription pad.

"Either way, whether it's bronchitis or pneumonia, this prescription should do the trick," he added with a friendly smile.

I left his office around 10:30 A.M., drove through the pharmacy and dropped off my prescription. Fortunately, the radiologist's office was right across the street.

I can go in and get the X-ray while my prescription is filled, so I can still get home in plenty of time and rest a few hours before afternoon carpool. Perfect!

Walking across the parking lot, I spoke out loud, "No matter what, Linda, you're going to be fine."

I stopped dead in my tracks and shook my head. I wasn't in the habit of talking to myself. My hands felt a little clammy and my breathing was labored. Puzzled, I realized I was trying to calm myself down. I smiled and shrugged, wondering where my concern was really coming from. Then I laughed it off.

Stop being so dramatic. It's just an X-ray to make sure I don't have pneumonia.

No one else was in the waiting room. I checked in with the receptionist and then sat down with a magazine.

"Linda," the nurse called.

Quickly, I jumped up and followed her into one of those cold, sterile rooms that made taking off my clothes the last thing I wanted to do.

"You can change in this room," she said. "Please remove your bra and put on the gown. Meet me in the room next door when you're ready. We will only be taking X-rays of your chest today."

I was shivering as I changed into the gown.

It's freezing in this place. I just want to get in my warm bed and go back to sleep.

Hurriedly, I walked into the X-ray room, hoping to get in and out as quickly as possible.

"How's the weather out there?" the nurse asked as she showed me where to stand in front of the machine.

"It looks like we might get some rain today," I responded. "But I can't complain. We had nice weather yesterday for Mother's Day. Our neighborhood opened up the pool."

"Do you have kids?" she asked.

"I do! I have a daughter, Megan. She's nine."

She interrupted me. "Okay, hold your breath while I take this picture." Then, continuing the small talk no doubt designed to make me feel comfortable, she asked, "What kinds of things does she like to do?"

I was a little irritated that she asked a question right after she told me to hold my breath. It's just like being at the dentist's office. They try to have a conversation with you when it's impossible to talk; meanwhile, you're wondering the whole time when the right time to talk would be.

"Well, she's a little artist, like my mom. It's one of those things that definitely skipped a generation—I can't even draw a straight line." I laughed. "But Megan is naturally talented like my mom. Her drawings amaze me. You would think she had drawing lessons. Her art is beautiful."

The nurse who had been encouraging all the chit-chat suddenly went dead silent.

This is weird, I thought. *Did I say something to upset her? Maybe she doesn't really want to hear about my child.*

Her next question caught me a little off guard.

"Has your back been hurting long?"

My heart skipped a beat, because my middle back *had* been hurting. I remembered complaining to Todd just a few weeks ago how much it was hurting while I was cooking dinner.

"Do you see something?"

I had forgotten for a split second why I was there. Suddenly I remembered that I was there because I had coughed up blood. Dr. Bauer's concern flashed in my mind again.

"Oh, no, just a routine question," the nurse answered.

She backed away without looking at me directly, and said, "Go ahead and change back into your clothes, and then have a seat in the back waiting area. The radiologist will be out shortly to talk with you."

As I grabbed my clothes to get dressed quickly, I knocked my purse over, spilling its contents onto the floor. Hands trembling slightly, I shoved my makeup case and wallet back into my purse.

Why would the radiologist want to talk with me? Don't they usually just send a letter in the mail saying everything is okay?

I swallowed hard. *She must have seen something on my X-ray.*

Alone in the patient waiting area in the back, I sat down and rubbed my hands together. My palms were sweaty again. For the first time, I took notice of how much I struggled to take a deep breath and realized that this had been going on for a while.

Something was wrong. Very wrong.

The wait felt like an eternity.

What if something is really wrong with me? What if I'm really sick? What if I die?

I drew a deep breath, told myself to calm down.

Okay, that's totally stupid! I only have a cold. It's not a big deal.

But all the "what-ifs" fueled more panic.

When the young radiologist with dark hair and glasses came in, I glanced at the clock. It was close to 11:30 A.M. As I gazed up to meet his eyes, I knew instantly he had devastating news.

My world stopped. The faces of my husband and my daughter came into my mind. Tears began streaming down my face.

"Linda, you have a ten-centimeter mass behind your heart," the radiologist said. "We need to take you back for a CAT scan right now to find out what else is going on. I've already called your doctor for him to write the order."

I was in too much shock to ask any questions. I could think of only one thing: I didn't want to be alone. My head was spinning.

Trying to fight back the tears I asked the radiologist, in a shaky voice, if I could call my husband.

"I just don't want to be here alone," I pleaded.

"Of course," he reassured me. "Take as much time as you need."

I ran out of the office building, frantically digging through my purse for my phone. My hands were trembling so badly I could barely dial my husband's number. Rays of sunshine were starting to beam through the clouds by this time, but I did not notice the warmth from the sun on my face.

"Todd, they've found something behind my heart! There's something wrong! There's something behind my heart!" I screamed frantically.

"Where are you? What do you mean there's something behind your heart?" my always-calm husband asked.

"I'm at the radiologist's. They took a chest X-ray and found something behind my heart. They have to do a scan to find out what is wrong with me," I explained, frustrated at having to slow down and explain. I needed to not be alone.

"Okay, okay, I'm on my way now, honey. It's going to be okay," he reassured me.

Not wanting to go back in, I called my mom, who lives two hours away. "Momma, they found something behind my heart. I thought I just had a cold. I'm scared. They need to do a CAT scan now." I started to cry again.

"Who needs to do a scan? Where are you? What is wrong?"

Mom didn't know I had been sick for the last week. I had to slow down again and explain it all over once more.

"It's going to be okay, sweetie. I know you're scared, but you're going to be okay. I promise you," she said calmly, but I could hear the worried rush in her voice. "We can get through this. I'm on my way."

I hung up the phone and retraced the very steps I had made just a half hour earlier, back through the parking lot and into the radiologist's office. As I did, the words I had said to myself echoed in my mind. *No matter what, Linda, you're going to be okay.*

At the time, I had figured that was just me talking to myself again. Now, I wondered. And finally it occurred to me to pray. It's just like me to remember to turn to God when suddenly I find myself alone with nowhere else to turn. *Lord, please tell me I'm going to be okay. I'm so scared.*

I didn't want to re-enter the radiologist's office. People in scrubs were passing by as I stood at the entrance outside. I noticed the heat from the sun beating against my back as an elderly couple slowly made their way through the heavy doors.

Is this it? Am I going to die? Lord, please let me erase today and start over. I only have a cold. I can take some cough medicine and get over this. I promise. I don't want to go back in there—why did I even come?

The staff was waiting for me, ready to prep me and proceed with the CAT scan. No need for a gown this time. The machine could see through anything.

"Mrs. Kuhar, lie down on the table, and we will get an IV started," instructed a different technician. This lady was in no mood for friendly chitchat like the nurse I had earlier. "We are going to run radioactive dye throughout your body to take a few pictures."

The technician poked and prodded to find a vein and then called in a coworker for assistance. Thankful to see a different nurse—one who might not have to poke and prod quite so much—walk in the room, I recognized her as the mother of one of Megan's classmates. What a relief to see a familiar face. She sweetly talked with me about everything under the sun, except the reality of why I was there. In her first attempt, she found a vein.

Everyone cleared the room and I was all alone.

Lying helplessly on the icy, sterile surface, I waited to be scanned. My heart cried out to God, *Lord, say something now, please! Anything. I just need to hear you.*

I'm not sure if I actually expected to hear God or not, but I heard the still, small voice the Bible tells me I can trust.

I endured the nails.

The quiet, calm answer gave me some peace. In my most vulnerable and fearful state of mind, he spoke, "I endured the nails."

A tear trickled down my cheek.

"Thank you, Jesus. Thank you." I exhaled a sigh of relief.

Somehow, in that desperate moment, I believed everything was going to be okay, whether I lived or died. No matter what pain or suffering I might go through, everything was okay, because Jesus had already done it all for me. He had conquered death—I had nothing to fear. God was with me then and throughout eternity.

Suddenly confident in the midst of the panic I had been feeling ever since the X-ray nurse mentioned back pain, I stopped trembling. I no longer had to fight back the tears. I had Jesus.

When the scan was over, the nurse came back into the room. Smiling, she said with a soft, gentle voice, "You have someone here for you. I believe it's your husband."

∾ ∾ ∾

Just a few hours earlier, I had kissed Todd goodbye as he left for a routine day at the bank. Now, we approached each other with apprehension. He stood up and wrapped his sturdy arms around me, comforting me as I rested my head securely on his chest. Our hearts burst with relief to kiss each other one more time. We held hands tightly and waited for the radiologist to meet with us.

It was 1 P.M. and we were back in the same waiting room as before. I really did not like this waiting area. With its straight, hard chairs and drab gray walls, it now felt like an ominous place, isolated from the part of the world where people were healthy and life goes on as planned. I hoped this time I would receive better news. I didn't know how it could get any worse.

It had been a little over an hour since I called my mom. I really wished she were already there. Todd and I didn't say a word to each other. We had been through so many doctor appointments while his mother was sick with cancer. This felt way too familiar and incredibly unreal at the same time. Surely, surely this couldn't be happening again.

After ten excruciating minutes, the radiologist came out to give us the news.

"Linda has a ten-centimeter mass behind her heart, as well as abnormalities in her lower abdomen and neck," the radiologist said.

"What does this mean? What does she have? How can this be treated?" Todd drilled him.

"We are scheduling an appointment with a surgeon as soon as possible to take a biopsy of her lymph nodes to determine the diagnosis," he answered.

No one mentioned the "C" word. It was in the back of my mind, but I was fighting to keep it out of my thoughts.

I'm only thirty-four years old, I thought. *This has to be some kind of strange infection I can get rid of with antibiotics, or some benign cysts that surgery will take care of.*

Of course. That must be it.

"How soon will we find out the results?" Todd asked.

I sat quietly, my mind stunned and racing at the same time.

"Depending on scheduling and labs, we should have the diagnosis within two weeks."

Two weeks! The words went through me like a physical shock. *I can't wait two weeks to find out what the heck is in my body!*

Panic, confusion, heartache.

I'm not waiting two weeks to find out if I'm dying! He's crazy. Has he lost his mind? I need to know today!

We sank back in our chairs, unable to move, feeling as if life as we knew it had been snatched right out of our hands.

The radiologist proceeded to give us more information, but looking back now, I'm pretty certain he could tell by the blank stare on our faces that we were not retaining or processing anything he was saying. He kindly stopped overloading us with information and handed us a card with his cell number.

"Please call me any time at this number, and I will be happy to answer any questions you might have. I know this is a lot to take in unexpectedly. I'm very sorry."

With deep sighs and tear-stained faces, we thanked him and left the building.

This time I walked through the parking lot hugging Todd tightly, wanting to never let him go. No words; just two hearts beating—surely we wouldn't be limited to the twenty years we'd already had together. Surely we had a long life together ahead of us.

Todd and I had been together almost our entire life. We started dating when we were fourteen years old, and got married when we were nineteen. We were young and naïve when we said I do. Most people thought we would never last, but Todd's parents believed in us, maybe because they, too, had been high school sweethearts.

Todd and his family had been a lifeline to sanity and stability for me after a childhood that had at times been traumatic. With his family of origin as the inspiration, we made it a point to live a Christian life. We became members of the United Methodist church around the corner from our house after our little girl was born. We raised Megan in the church. I volunteered in the church office, taught Sunday school, and led home Bible studies. I thought my faith was solid because I was doing all the right "Christian" things.

Surely, God would reward those efforts.

Our marriage by no means had been a fairy tale. We definitely had some rocky times, but by God's grace we were able to make it through.

"You're in no condition to drive, honey," Todd said. "Why don't you ride in my car?"

I didn't want to leave his side no matter what, so I got into his car.

My cell phone rang. It was Mom, letting me know she was ten minutes away.

"Meet us at Pei Wei Restaurant. It's just across the street from the radiologist's office. We just got into the car," I told her.

The second I saw my mom walk into the restaurant I ran to her. There's nothing in the world like your momma when life falls apart. I was relieved to fall into her hug. Mom was in charge now. The weight was no longer all on my shoulders. Somehow my momma was going to make this all right. Mom, being the confident woman that she is, reassured us that everything was going to be okay. Her rock-solid, take-charge attitude allowed my mind to calm momentarily.

Sipping on our tea, Todd and I tried to recall everything the radiologist told us, but we remembered the story differently.

"She only has a mass behind her heart, nothing else," Todd said.

"No, honey, he said I have 'things' in my abdomen and neck," I corrected him.

We went back and forth for a few minutes.

Mom finally said, "Why don't we just go back and talk with the radiologist so that we have all the facts?"

Todd and I agreed. We were so confused and everything felt surreal—like we were in a dream.

At this point, it was time to pick up Megan from school, so Todd left to get her. Mom and I headed back to the radiologist's office. Begrudgingly, with very slow steps, I walked back through the parking lot and into the office for the third time that day. This time, my mom had enough strength for both of us.

The doctor wasn't surprised in the least to see me again.

"Hi, Doctor, this is my mom, Alta," I said, after we were once again sitting in that back waiting room I had already learned to hate. "Do you mind explaining to her what you shared with my husband and me? We were very confused after we left. The two of us have different understandings of what might be going on."

"Sure, let's go back into my office where I can pull up the scans for you and show you exactly what I see."

Entering the tiny dark room, he offered us a seat, but I refused to sit. I stood there with my arms crossed—guarded as if I could protect myself from what he was about to reveal. Mom, on the other hand, sat down with him and made herself comfortable. Four big screens lit up with black and white images of my torso and abdomen.

The radiologist pointed to the screen.

"The gray areas here and here are the abnormalities in her abdomen," he explained to Mom, as I stood there, bewildered.

"You can see in her neck that she has many more there as well. This is her heart and, as you can see, this gray area shows there is a mass behind it."

Mom began to fire off her questions. "Do you think she has cancer? What type of cancer? How will it be treated? What is her life expectancy?"

She was relentless, as any mother would be.

Hearing the word *cancer* from my mother's lips was more than I could bear. I ran out of the room crying. I made it back outside to the parking lot and called my best friend on the phone.

"Catherine, I have cancer! What is happening to me! I think I have cancer!!"

Sobbing and yelling into the phone at the top of my lungs, I dropped to my knees and fell face down. Asphalt scraped my elbows and knees. Two men stopped their cars—one older gentleman in a suit and another younger man driving a pickup.

"Miss, are you okay?" the older gentleman said, concern in his voice.

"Should I call the EMTs?" the other man said.

At first I didn't respond—I couldn't find my voice. Finally, I looked up at both of them and just shook my head no.

"I think I have cancer," I whimpered softly.

"I'm so sorry, ma'am," said the younger man.

Sorry for what? I thought. *Sorry that I might be dying?*

There's not a more helpless feeling in the world. Not having any control over an unidentifiable disease running rampant through your body, not knowing if you're going to die.

I sat on the hard, rocky asphalt until I heard my mom's voice coming from behind me.

"Come on, honey, let's go home."

I don't want to go home. How can I go home?

Devastated and afraid, I thought of something just as scary as the prospect of cancer: telling my little girl the news of my illness. I did not want to face my little girl's bright-green eyes. Megan is my everything. Her world had already been turned upside down by losing her Grammy to cancer. How could I rock her world with news that I, too, might have cancer?

I just couldn't do it.

Mom got into her car and I got into mine.

I turned the radio off and drove in silence. *How was this possible? How could I have cancer?* Stopping at a red light I stared into space. *Maybe it's not cancer? Oh, Lord, please don't let me have cancer. I am only thirty-four years old. I have a life to live. I am not ready to die. My baby girl needs her momma.*

The next thing I heard was the car behind me honking. The light had turned green. Looking up in my rearview mirror, I could see a lady angrily waving her hands around in the air at me.

By the time Mom and I arrived home, Todd had taken Megan across the street to a friend's house for a playdate.

Thank God. I was not emotionally prepared to see my curli-cued little angel.

I plopped down in the same chair where I had placed the phone call to the doctor's office that morning—a lifetime ago, it felt. Looking around the room, everything seemed different. Family photos hanging above the fireplace had a whole new meaning. Megan's backpack sitting in the corner was like a punch in the stomach. And, incongruously, the sun was now out, brightening the room.

Megan.

Will I be here to see her grow up?

Eternity lingered in the air.

Todd and I sat staring at each other with shock plastered across our faces as we tried hard to be optimistic.

Mom spoke up in a sincere, soft voice. "Linda, next year at this time all of this will be behind all of us. We are going on a journey, but we will come through it, and it will be just a memory."

Her words were comforting and frustrating at the same time. *I don't want to go on a journey! I don't want to be sick. I don't do sick.* My fear began to turn to anger. The thought of not having control infuriated me. *I'm a healthy person! I have too many things to do. I don't have time to be sick.*

Later that night when Meg came home from her playdate, we pretended everything was okay. We told her Nana had come down for the day for a surprise visit. Every time I looked at Meg, I thought my spirit might be dying as well as my body. Walking with Meg upstairs to her bedroom, I felt a lump in my throat. I choked back the tears as I kissed those rosy-red cheeks good-night. I wanted that moment to last for the rest of my life.

On that May evening on the day after Mother's Day, tucking in my little girl felt almost sacred.

That night felt as if it had to be the longest night of my entire life. Tossing and turning in my bed every five minutes, I dozed off for a little bit, only to wake up in a pool of sweat, my pajamas soaking wet.

Night sweats, I would soon learn, are a sign of cancer. I'd been having sweats for months, but never thought anything of it. Now, I wondered, and began to think of other changes I'd been experiencing in my body in recent months. Even though it hadn't been officially diagnosed, suddenly this cancer thing was becoming more and more real to me.

My crying woke up Todd.

"This cannot be real!" I whispered hoarsely. "This cannot be happening to me. I'm so scared. What are we going to do?"

I was definitely angry. Words began to come out of my mouth that were anything but godly. *When am I going to wake up from this hell?*

Shaking my head, I paced the floors in our bedroom, crying, cursing, and yelling. Thank goodness Megan's bedroom was upstairs, far away from ours. After my tantrum, I crumpled in my husband's arms and buried my face in his chest.

"I'm really scared, honey. Really, really scared."

I had learned to be a pretty strong person in a crisis. But this was different from anything I'd ever experienced. It felt like an out-of-body experience, as if I had a starring role in a real-life horror movie. I wanted desperately to push the pause button, but there was no escape. Paralyzed with fear of the unknown, I lay helpless in Todd's arms for the rest of the night.

I did not pray. I was all out of words.

CHAPTER THREE

Waiting

FOR TWO DAYS, I WAS on autopilot.

Wednesday was the day of the biopsy. I couldn't eat. I couldn't drink anything after midnight. Not that it mattered. I was so nervous that nothing would have stayed down.

I wasn't scared about the biopsy. I was terrified by the fact that I might be dying. After losing Judy to cancer, it didn't occur to me that I might be able to fight the battle and win. Cancer to me was a death sentence.

I tried to keep myself busy. I took Megan to school and drove back home, but I couldn't focus on anything. In truth, I was freaking out.

While I obsessed over the fact that I might be dying of cancer, I chain-smoked cigarettes on my front porch. It kept my hands busy. When I'm in the middle of a life-or-death crisis, I sometimes revert back to those old habits from high school. I was hoping that bad old habit of smoking would somehow calm my fears of the hell I was facing.

My mom, my friend Catherine, and I left about 3 P.M. Wednesday afternoon to go to the hospital for the outpatient procedure. Todd stayed home with Megan. We told her the doctor had to remove a sore on my neck but that it would be all better in a few weeks. That was as close to the truth as I could bring myself to come with my nine-year-old daughter.

The surgeon removed one lymph node near my collarbone to be sent off for diagnosis. The procedure itself took less than an hour, but for Mom and Catherine it seemed like hours.

Catherine and I had been friends for about nine years. We met when her son and my daughter were babies. We were more like sisters than friends—which meant we didn't always get along perfectly, but we always had each other's back no matter what. Having Catherine there along with my mother reassured me that I really was going to be okay. I mean, I couldn't bail on my friend, right? So of course I would get well.

While I was in recovery, the surgeon told Mom and Catherine the node did not look good due to its size and texture. He said he was hoping the lymph node would have been hard, indicating a less-serious cancer; instead, it was supple, more pliable to the touch. He said a lymph node should be about the size of a pinky fingernail; however, mine was larger than a golf ball. And it was wrapped around the jugular vein in my neck.

When I heard this news days later, I suddenly remembered a day about a year earlier. I was getting ready one morning, blow drying my hair, then pulling it up into a ponytail, when I noticed something in the mirror. Just below my left ear, a vein was bulging in my neck.

I made a face, thinking it was just one more reason to fret over something I didn't like about myself.

I had mentioned it to Todd, but didn't think much more about it. Maybe it would go away. Maybe I would just need to stop wearing so many ponytails so that my long hair would cover it.

Never in a million years did it occur to me that this was a sign I shouldn't ignore.

When I came out of the anesthesia, Mom did not tell me what the surgeon had said, because she knew it wasn't the right time for me to hear it. The surgeon told Mom and me that it would take about a week for the lab results to come in and that he would call us with a diagnosis. Then, we all would discuss the next steps.

Waiting. Waiting. Another week to wait.

❧ ❧ ❧

The weather was getting warmer. My family liked to do things outside when spring arrived. School would be ending soon, summer was on its way, and we loved going to the pool. We had a family beach vacation planned, and I didn't want anything to interfere with that.

Plus, Megan and I had a lot of mother-daughter time planned to hang out, go shopping, and pamper ourselves with mani-pedis during the summer ahead.

But now what was my summer going to look like? No trips? No fun? It loomed ahead like a dark cloud of doctor appointments, medicine that would make me sick, and treatments that would make me too weak to ignore being sick. Too sick and tired to take care of Megan and create memories with my family. In limbo—unable to schedule anything.

While my friends made plans for summer activities, I kept thinking I didn't even know if I would be alive come the Fourth of July.

For the week following the biopsy, Todd and I basically lived in anticipated misery. We tried to forget and just go about our routines. But, every time the phone rang, I would jump. I was antsy. I was agitated. It was a week of pure hell.

The perfect time to turn to God. Right?

I can only confess that at this point God was not in the forefront of my thinking. I was trying to figure out my life all on my own. Trying my hardest to control the outcome, which is humanly impossible. Cancer had become my only god, the thing that ran my life and determined my destiny.

We still had not told our little girl what was really going on. It was stressful keeping everything secret from Megan, but I did not want to tell her anything until I knew exactly what was wrong with me. She had already been through so much heartache after losing her Grammy. I couldn't stomach the thought of telling her I was sick, too. So my neighbor and friend, Sarah, who lived across the street, kindly kept Megan busy after school most days.

Megan wasn't the only one I couldn't be completely honest with. Several other friends knew that we were waiting to find out the results. When they called to offer their sympathy and support, I faked being strong and told them I was going to be okay.

Of course, I did what most patients do these days—and the complete opposite of what the surgeon told me. I surfed the Internet to find out what kind of cancer I had. I filled my head with horrific stories of what it might be and how long I might live. I quickly allowed the Internet to become another one of my gods, instead of actually turning to the God who really had the answers.

∾ ∾ ∾

Exactly a week after my biopsy, the phone rang.

I saw on caller ID that it was the doctor's office. This was it. The call I had been so eager to get, but also dreading.

I wanted the waiting to stop, but I didn't want to hear anything about cancer.

I wanted to know if I was dying, but I didn't want to know if I had to live with cancer.

When the phone rang that afternoon in May, Todd and I had been soaking in the glory of North Carolina's beautiful spring in our backyard. It was a perfect afternoon—a day too pretty to receive bad news. The fountain had been cleaned out and was bubbling close by; the daylilies planted by the porch were coming to life. The sun was shining, the temperatures warm enough to go sleeveless, although I could still feel the bandage on my neck where they had removed the lymph node. "Mrs. Kuhar, this is your surgeon, Dr. Weston. I've got good news and bad news for you."

"Really?" I smiled with relief.

"You have Hodgkin's lymphoma stage three cancer."

Excuse me? Good news? Is he crazy? I had read enough on the Internet to know that stage three is *never* good news. Stage three means the cancer has already started to spread. Stage three is the last stage before stage four get-your-affairs-in-order cancer.

"The reason this is good news," he continued, "is because when I did your biopsy, I thought it was a different type of cancer that is not curable, but Hodgkin's lymphoma is treatable and even curable. The bad news is, this *is* serious. We cannot wait. You need to see an oncologist right away."

He paused, no doubt to see if I had a question or a comment. I couldn't say a word.

The forced cheerfulness of his voice came over the phone line. "I have no doubt that you are a strong woman and will get through this, Mrs. Kuhar."

His optimism felt hollow. His words felt like a death sentence.

In shock, I dropped the phone. I collapsed in my husband's arms once again.

"I have cancer, honey. I have cancer."

We clung to each other and sobbed.

CHAPTER FOUR

Fear

I NOW LOOKED AT LIFE through the lens of cancer.

I'm not going to lie, cancer sucks! There's no way around it. I was scared, resentful, and pretty much pissed off. Everyone reacts to trauma differently. Some experience withdrawal, some deny, some get depressed. Some get livid and just about lose their ever-lovin' mind, and that was me.

The morning after my diagnosis, I went to Starbucks. As I was standing in line observing the hustle and bustle, I wanted to scream to the top of my lungs, *Look at all you people going on with your lives! This is not fair, I might die and all you are worried about is your stupid lattes and Frappuccinos. Give me a break!*

I was outraged that I was now part of the "cancer club."

I don't deserve this.

Crossing my arms tightly and clenching my fists as I waited for my coffee, I was annoyed by all the people standing in line.

I'm too young. I have a life to live. My friends are planning summer getaways, and I'm planning how to survive.

I glanced over and saw my reflection in the glass window with the silhouette of my long hair flowing down my back. The long hair that would most likely be gone soon, lost to chemotherapy.

This is not fair! Why me?

Todd and I realized there was no way around it. We had to tell Meg the truth.

The last week had been a series of little white lies to try and keep some sort of normalcy in our home. She was only nine years old and a little too young, in my opinion, to have her own cell phone; however, with everything that was getting ready to take place in the coming months we thought it would be wise for her to have her own phone. That way she could reach us anytime, anywhere.

I planned exactly how I was going to break the news to her. It was going to be subtle. I was going to reassure her that everything was going to be all right. Instead, it just happened.

Meg and I were sitting outside of the AT&T store on a bench while Todd finished up purchasing and activating her new phone. She was so excited that she had just picked out her very first cell phone. This made her feel like a grown-up. Something struck me in that moment, looking in those innocent eyes as the sunshine shimmered in her hair.

It was time to tell her.

"Meg, Mommy has something to tell you."

Looking up at me with sad eyes, she said, "You have cancer, don't you?"

I was stunned, overcome with shock. Clearly, as so many people have said over the years, you can't keep anything from children. They have ways of knowing. I had a moment of regret, wondering how long my precious girl had carried this fear in secret.

I forced myself to speak calmly. "Well . . . uh . . . yes, honey. I do. But Mommy is going to be okay. I promise."

She looked down into her lap, then stared straight into my eyes. "Are you going to die like Grammy?"

This was not how I had anticipated our conversation going. It had been planned out much better in my mind. "No, I am not going to die like Grammy. Grammy had a cancer that could not be cured, so no matter how much medicine she took, she was going to die. My cancer is different. All I have to do is take the medicine and I will get better. I promise you."

She did not look entirely convinced. And I knew my little girl well enough to know that she always tried hard to contain her feelings and put up a good front. It would be a long time before I realized how much she hid her anxiety during this time—because she wanted to make sure everyone focused on helping me get well instead of helping her cope.

I pulled Megan tightly to my chest and squeezed her. I kissed the top of her head. My heart pleaded with God. *Lord, please let me raise my baby girl. She needs her momma. Please.*

∾ ∾ ∾

Two days after the dreaded phone call from my surgeon, Todd and I met with an oncologist. Meeting him for the first time was nerve-racking. My life was now in this doctor's hands—at least, that's how it felt. As if he had the control switch to whether I'd live or die.

As Todd and I sat on the other side of the doctor's desk, he gave us, in a very matter-of-fact voice, all the details of what the next six months might look like.

"Linda will have a total of twelve rounds of chemo, followed by around twenty to thirty rounds of radiation," he said. "We use steroids to help patients with nausea and vomiting. Many patients experience fewer side effects if they take steroids. However, you will be on a drug that will cause your hair to fall out. That is one of the hardest parts of therapy for female patients."

It was what it was. I really felt like I had no say in the matter. Never mind waiting for chemotherapy, I wanted to vomit right then. I kept looking at the trash can, just in case. Thank God for my husband. Todd is analytical and was able to gather all the facts without going into a frenzy. He kept asking detailed questions while taking lots of notes so that he could go back home and do his research.

Me, on the other hand, I'm a feeler. I don't care to know all the facts. I just want to know the outcome so I can decide how to react emotionally. In this case, I wanted to know if I was going to live and, if not, how much time I had left. Typically I react before fully processing information, and the more facts that were presented that day, the angrier I got. My life was unraveling minute by minute and there was nothing I could do.

How could this be happening to me? Just a few weeks ago I was going about my everyday life, dealing with the normal pressures of being a wife and mother. And now cancer?

All of a sudden I remembered how I'd been popping ibuprofen like it was candy over the last month. I'd not been feeling like myself for some time, but you know how it is when you're so busy with life and taking care of family. As women, we tend to put ourselves on the back burner.

The next week consisted of a PET scan, bone marrow biopsy, and surgery to have a Port-a-Cath—a small medical appliance installed beneath the skin to give easy access to veins—placed in my chest for chemotherapy. The PET scan and bone marrow biopsy would show if the cancer had spread into my bone marrow yet. If it had, this would mean my cancer was at stage four and more invasive treatments would be required. Statistics for a full recovery would change, too.

Either way, my first round of chemotherapy would begin the following week.

More waiting, wondering, hoping, and praying. *Lord, please let my cancer be at a stage three and not stage four.*

I was scheduled to receive twelve chemo treatments. That meant going to the oncologist every other Friday starting in late June 2009. I pulled out my calendar, marking the days I was scheduled for treatment. This gave me some sort of control over my life, a little sense of satisfaction. Chemo one, chemo two, chemo three, chemo four, chemo five . . . all the way to chemo twelve, spelled out perfectly on my datebook. I could count down my treatments one by one and move on with my life.

I had to control it myself because I surely was not giving it to God to the run the show. This was my job, or so I thought.

Linda's plan was that by November I would have my final round of chemotherapy and then move on to radiation, as long as I was still in stage three.

This was going to work out well because, based on Linda's plan, I would not be going through chemo at Christmas. I could still have the family over for our traditional Christmas dinner and gift exchange.

My goal was to ring in the 2010 New Year with this whole cancer thing behind me. What a celebration that would be!

I had long forgotten, or perhaps never really learned, that God's plans aren't always the same as my plans.

∿ ∿ ∿

D-Day, the first day of chemotherapy.

What a helpless feeling. I was disgusted that I had to go sit in a room for half the day and be juiced up with toxic chemicals that were somehow going to save my life by poisoning not just the cancer cells in my body, but the healthy cells, as well. What irony was that? I might as well have played Russian roulette. I felt violated. My life and my body were out of my control.

To get out the anger and rage I was feeling, I knew I needed some sort of emotional release.

Years prior to this whole cancer diagnosis ordeal I had been in therapy, dealing with depression and anxiety. The tools I learned in counseling, such as emotional-release exercises, taught me how to process emotions that are trapped inside the body instead of stuffing them deep inside.

Shortly before chemo was scheduled to begin, I knew I had to process what I was feeling or I was going to explode.

So I headed over to the home of one of my very best friends, Linda Huddleston. Linda and I had been friends for more than six years. She is the type of friend I can be completely real with. When I'm with her, I'm relaxed and carefree. I feel safe with her. She doesn't judge me or think I'm weird. Anytime I hang out with her, I'm naturally able to let out all of my authentic emotions—even the most ugly—and she doesn't think I'm crazy. She exudes empathy and compassion.

That morning before my first chemo treatment, Linda knew exactly what I needed. When I arrived at her front door, she grabbed my hand and took me around her house to her backyard. There sat an old, ragged, wooden rocking chair with a baseball bat propped up beside it.

She looked at me and chuckled. "Want to take it out of its misery?"

"Oh girl, you know I do!"

We carried the chair to the middle of her yard and threw it down. I took the bat over my shoulder, ready to beat the living daylights out of that chair. Bam!

The first hit barely made a crack in it.

I swung again. Bam!

The back of the chair cracked right down the middle.

"Yes!" I screamed. My heart was racing with a thrill of excitement as I kept swinging.

"I hate cancer! Cancer sucks! I hate you!"

My hands were getting sweaty, but I tightened my grip and kept hitting. "You are not going to kill me, cancer! I will beat you!"

I pounded the seat. Wood starting flying off, but the chair was tougher than we'd imagined. It wasn't yet destroyed, just damaged.

Linda stepped in and turned the chair on its side so I could get a better angle.

Hitting it as hard as I possibly could, I felt the vibration run throughout my body. I kept pounding. Sweat dripped from my brow. My wrists began to hurt from the impact. I kept going.

I beat that poor chair until there was nothing left in me. With arms trembling and weak, I handed the bat to Linda. She happily took the bat and finished the job.

The chair was a mess. Chunks of wood were strewn across her yard. A small pile of splinters rested on the grass at our feet. We'd killed the chair.

I felt like I'd killed the cancer.

Most importantly, my anger was gone. I felt a huge release of negative emotions and helplessness. I wasn't helpless. I'd beaten the crap out of that rocking chair!

I hugged Linda, feeling spent but free of the fear. Looking across the yard, we noticed her neighbor peering over the fence. This lady had witnessed the entire rocker-bashing ceremony. We stood briefly there like two kids caught with their hands in the cookie jar, then we fell to the ground laughing and hugging each other, getting grass stains all over my yoga pants.

I didn't care. If I could batter that chair into splinters, what chance did cancer have?

∾ ∾ ∾

Heading back home after releasing those negative emotions, I found myself in the most tranquil state I had experienced since that fateful Monday after Mother's Day.

I was ready to talk with God.

I stopped at one of the many quaint parks in my neighborhood. This one was just around the corner from my house, with a few benches tucked under the trees and some playground equipment surrounded by neatly trimmed shrubs. It was quiet that morning, like an outdoor sanctuary under a canopy of trees. Sitting against a sprawling shade tree, clasping my hands, I bowed until my head fell between my knees. Tears trickled to the ground. For the first time since all this chaos began, I was finally ready to hand it over to God. I was ready to give up control and fully let it go—at least for that day.

I only had five simple words to pray: "Lord, your will be done."

My weakness poured out through my tears. They weren't hysterical tears, either. They were cleansing tears. Tears of surrender and trust, even in the midst of fear. That simple prayer had come from the deepest part of me. After saying those words, I knew I was okay.

Fifteen minutes or more passed as I sat there and cried.

Finally, I felt at rest in the quiet, listening to the birds chirping as the gentle breeze brushed against the back of my neck. The grass felt cool beneath the palms of my hands. I tasted salt where tears dried at the corners of my mouth. My eyes felt swollen but clear.

I could have stayed in that spot for the rest of my life.

As much release as I felt, I still did not want to get up. I still did not want to go to chemotherapy.

Peace washed over me as I slowly stood and returned to my car and made my way home to meet Todd.

I knew this was a battle I had to fight, but I had finally remembered I was not fighting it alone. I had God on my side.

Before Todd and I got in the car to go to my first chemo appointment, I looked up to the sky, as blue and clear as a painting. I felt God affirming my strength to go through the treatment and my determination to get better. It wasn't my confidence. It was a "Godfidence" to fight the fight.

‿ ‿ ‿

On the ride to my appointment, I told Todd all about Linda's gift of the emotional-release ceremony. Todd got a kick out of the story. We laughed and held hands the whole way to the doctor's office.

The infusion center was located inside my oncologist's office, which was just a short distance from home. Recliners were lined up against the walls of the treatment room. The room was freezing cold and had a strange odor. Frail patients with IVs hooked to their ports were covered in blankets. Expressions of desperation loomed. I felt sick at my stomach.

How can this be my life? I'm only thirty-four. This feels like an old-folks home. These people look like they are waiting here to die.

A few patients welcomed me, as they could tell it was my first day. An elderly lady shriveled up in her chair and covered by a fluffy quilted blanket was barely able to lift her hand, but she waved. A gentleman dressed in bedroom slippers and a gray sweat suit five sizes too big kindly leaned forward to greet me. The expression in their eyes appeared helpless.

It felt like a war zone. I thought I was going to throw up. I felt so out of place and wasn't convinced that I belonged there.

My nurse was about the same age as me, a funny and sweet woman with short red hair. Her spunky, take-charge personality helped me feel confident that she knew exactly what she was doing. She settled me in my chair as she explained the routine and my first chemo she was about to administer.

"It will take about a half hour to an hour for each drug," she said. "You have four different chemotherapy drugs, so it might take over four hours. Plan on five hours for each appointment to be on the safe side."

Then she proceeded to inject me with the first chemo. This chemo was red, and when it enters your veins, it can sometimes burn. It has many side effects, such as hair loss, mouth sores, low blood counts—even congestive heart failure.

No wonder they call it the "red devil."

Once the nurse left, I looked over at my husband, and for the first time ever in our marriage I felt like a burden. I feared that I would be draining, that he might get weary of a sick and helpless wife who could no longer be super mom. I worried that he might find me repulsive when I had no hair, no energy, and was incapable of doing normal things like cooking or caring for our daughter.

Sitting there, waiting for the red devil to drip into my veins, I was more afraid of the aftermath than the actual treatment itself.

◌ ◌ ◌

Most of my treatments were manageable. The worst side effects were from the steroids.

Thanks to the steroids I often could not sleep a wink. And they blew me up like a balloon. I gained more than fifty pounds. None of my clothes fit—not even my shoes! I looked like the Michelin Tire man. That was depressing in itself.

I thought I would lose weight going through chemo, not gain it.

I stayed up all hours of the night that summer, sitting on my front porch counting stars or journaling on CaringBridge, a blog site that allows family and friends to stay up-to-date during a health crisis such as cancer. My friend Catherine, who somehow always knew exactly the right thing to do at exactly the right moment, had set it up for me. It was a wonderful way for me to share how I was dealing with cancer, keep my friends up-to-date, and ask for prayers, especially during those dark times when I was feeling so afraid. It also made life much easier for Todd and me. We didn't have to keep repeating ourselves to friends over and over again. It kept the phone from ringing incessantly. The absolute best part of CaringBridge was the outpouring of love in the comments from friends and loved ones. The love, prayers, and support everyone poured out to me gave me strength to keep fighting. They were my inspiration.

My motto during that time became FROG—Fully Rely On God. It gave me—well, all of us, really—hope and reassurance that God was in control. I signed every journal entry with FROG and even had froggie art all over my CaringBridge page. Friends sent me gifts and cards with frogs, reminding me we were all standing in agreement as we fully relied on God.

During those wee hours of the morning, while I was all alone and the rest of the world was quietly sleeping, I felt truly connected to the Lord. I relied on him like never before in my life. I wrestled with fears of not being around to watch my daughter grow up, graduate from high school, or walk down the aisle with her daddy on her wedding day. I imagined grandchildren I might never see and not growing old with my husband. Countless tears were shed as I rocked back and forth through the long summer nights on my front porch. Many silent prayers were spoken.

Even though I was tiptoeing the line between heaven and earth, desperately hoping to stay a while longer with my family, my soul knew that heaven was the ultimate goal. In the stillness of the night, my heart sang with a broken hallelujah.

When panic gripped me, I refused to let my mind linger in the unknown. Instead of trying to fight off anxiety and worry, I took it captive and compared it with what God had to say in his Word: "I will not die but live, and will proclaim what the LORD has done" (Ps. 118:17).

Minute by minute I was challenged with what I was going to choose to believe, fear or faith.

CHAPTER FIVE

Heart

WHILE MANY PEOPLE WAKE UP on Friday mornings looking forward to the start of their weekends, during chemo I always woke up anticipating, at best, insurmountable fatigue, painful mouth sores, and a debilitating lack of appetite.

The first chemo treatment was just as the doctor said it would be. I really did not feel anything different while I was sitting in the chair getting juiced up. But when I got home, it hit me. As soon as I walked through the front door, I ran to the bathroom and got sick. The nausea subsided after an hour or so.

The first appointment was emotionally exhausting for both Todd and me. The whole experience was draining, something we never imagined going through when we at nineteen shared our vows about "in sickness or in health." Maybe having a little cold and serving chicken noodle soup to each other in bed, but not this. We were too young to feel like we were in a geriatrics unit.

That first night Todd fell fast asleep like a baby.

I didn't sleep a wink.

After the first wave of nausea subsided, I spent the next twenty-four hours flying high. Pumped up with steroids, I was suddenly full of energy. I ran around the house organizing and cleaning like a crazy woman.

That night, while Todd slept, I sat on the front porch thinking, praying, wishing, and hoping I would have more time with my family. It was a warm night and the moon was bright. The neighborhood was sound asleep. I, on the other hand, swayed back and forth in my old rickety rocking chair with a candle lit. I was the only one on the block showing any signs of life. Then again, they could afford to sleep. They had plenty of time. They would wake up for years to come, with all the time in the world to love people, play with their kids, make up for all the things they'd gotten wrong.

Is this gonna be it? My thirty-four years of life paraded slowly and bleakly before my eyes.

I wished I could get the time back. All those days worrying about silly, trivial things. All of it meaningless.

God, please give me more time with Todd and Megan. I want to do more with my life.

I had taken so much for granted.

Lord, all I've ever wanted to do was love hurting people in the world. I haven't done enough of that. Lord, forgive me. I feel like I've wasted my life. I could have done more. I can do more. I will do more, if you give me a chance, Lord.

❧ ❧ ❧

The next day, with no sleep and the steroids fading fast, the fatigue set in. I slept all day.

The first full week after chemo was as normal as could be expected. Taking care of Megan, coffee with girlfriends, and lots of journaling and praying. Also lots of cussing and going to therapy sessions to process my reality. I was thankful I didn't have a full-time career, so I could stay in my jammies on the days I felt too tired or depressed to get out of the house.

The next chemo session loomed ahead. Dreading what might happen to me, I was lost inside my thoughts. Depression set in.

Sitting and waiting to be injected with chemo was a very lonely feeling. Like nobody in the world had a clue as to what I was going through. Friends wanted to come over and distract me, but my mind couldn't focus.

Is the chemo going to work? Will it really save me? I can't believe this is what my life has turned into . . . helplessly awaiting doctor appointments and chemotherapy.

Friends who read my CaringBridge site, though, probably saw me as confident and strong, clinging to God every second.

Tuesday, May 19, 2009, 11:00 A.M.

Hi, friends! Just wanted to say thank you so much for all of your love and support. God is so good and I trust him completely. Hope everyone is having a great day and enjoying the sunshine, because I think we will be getting some rain for a few days soon.

Love, hugs, and kisses,
Linda (Fully Rely On God)

Saturday, May 30, 2009, 5:15 A.M.

Thank you all for your comments on my site. I read them over and over and cry most of the time because I'm so overwhelmed by your kindness, love, and support in my life. Each one of you will never know what your words mean to me. Thank you! Feeling pretty normal this morning considering how crazy the last two weeks have been. I believe God has been listening to each of your prayers, and he continues to bless me over and over. Thank you!

Love, peace, and joy always in Jesus Christ,
Linda (Fully Rely On God)

Wednesday, June 10, 2009, 7:53 A.M.

I feel very confident that God is going to heal me 100 percent from cancer. He has given me a peace that surpasses all understanding and I trust this is exactly His plan for my life. He has much work for me to do to help other people, really just love other people to show everyone how truly special they are to him.

In His hands I am blessed,
Linda (Fully Rely On God)

What a lot of hooey!

I'm not saying I was lying when I posted on CaringBridge. When I was writing my posts, I did feel confident in God. I did trust that I was going to get through. In those moments, many of them during times of prayer and reflection in the dead of night when the rest of the world slept peacefully, I did fully rely on God.

But when I walked through the everyday-ness of life with cancer, my thoughts were still laced with fear, with dread, with depression.

Especially because I was a Christian, though, I believed I needed to keep up a strong and courageous facade. But I had many dark, lonely days I didn't tell anyone about. I was too sad to reach out to anyone for prayer or encouragement. I stayed in bed, drowning in self-pity. Isolated.

≈ ≈ ≈

One day when my mom came to Charlotte for a visit, she brought me a gift. Her eyes twinkled with excitement as she handed me the package. She could hardly wait for me to open it.

"When I saw this, I had to buy it for you."

I was excited too. I ripped the box open and found a plaque with the words "Believe in Miracles!" inscribed across it in bright, glittery gold letters.

It hit me more fully than it had up to that point: I had cancer. And healing—*surviving*—might require a lot more than modern medicine, well-trained doctors, chemotherapy, radiation, or surgery . . . or even willpower. Healing might require a miracle. And miracles were God's territory. Not the territory of doctors or science or the health-care industry.

Only God delivers miracles.

As strange as it may sound, day in and day out I went through bouts of denial. Having cancer is something I never fully wanted to accept.

Mom cleared off a shelf in my living room and propped up the new Believe in Miracles sign. It would become my frequent reminder that I was going to get through everything and that God was in control.

Some days I would look at that sign and trust it. Other days, the best I could manage was to stare at it and try to believe.

∿ ∿ ∿

A few days before my second chemo treatment, Todd and I were driving down the Interstate on our way to Ikea to browse and take our minds off everything. It was a sweet time because we were hanging on to each other's every word—like we were on our first date. Getting off at the exit and heading toward the store, we passed a Volkswagen dealership. The cutest little car caught my eye.

"I've always wanted one of those VW bug convertibles!" I said to Todd. "Someday I'd like to have one."

My husband looked over at me, smiling with those cute dimples and hazel-green eyes of his, and said, "Really? You want one?"

"Oh, honey, I'm just kidding. Maybe one day."

We drove on to Ikea and browsed through every inch of the store and checked out with a few storage bins and small items. Anything to keep our minds busy was a huge help.

I should have known that wouldn't be the end of my casual comment about wanting a VW convertible. Where I'm emotional and excitable, Todd is calm and faithful. He had approached the cancer the way he approached everything—with confidence that we would get through it. Todd was one person I could always rely on to love me unconditionally and to demonstrate that love generously.

As we approached the Volkswagen dealership on our way back home, Todd made a quick turn into the dealership lot. I was taken completely by surprise, but then I was reminded of what Todd's grandmother always had said: "When life gives you lemons, make lemonade."

A few hours later, after trading in the car we drove in with, we drove home with a cute black convertible VW bug with tan leather seats. With the top down and our hair blowing in the wind, we sang along with every song blaring on the radio. I was behind the wheel of my dream car and cancer was far from my mind.

After we got home, we gave Megan a ride in the convertible. She was in heaven. The wind blowing in her face, she giggled, raising her arms up in the air like riding on a roller coaster. "Mommy, this is so fun! I can't wait to take my friends on a ride with us."

I was finding out how my perspective on life could change when I lived like I was dying. I stopped procrastinating. I lived from my heart. I did what matters most. Said the words that were buried inside. I spent time with the ones I truly love.

Not always, of course. But sometimes.

That's what it was like on the good days. And even in the midst of receiving treatments and knowing I might be headed for my final days, there were good days.

Receiving so much love and support from others was new to me. Girlfriends drove me to my chemo treatments and sat with me. They spent countless hours taking care of me—pouring out words of encouragement, talking about everything else but cancer and chemo, and fetching ice chips and warm blankets.

My friend Sarah was an angel sent from heaven, not only because Megan spent countless days and nights at her house playing with her daughter, but also because she did so much for me. She tended to my physical needs as well as my emotional needs. Sarah restyled my bedroom into a sanctuary. She showed up on my doorstep numerous times with a homemade spa-in-a-bag, and she massaged my feet and painted my toenails (my favorite OPI color, Paint My Moji-toes Red!). I wasn't allowed to get a professional mani-pedi while undergoing chemo, due to the risk of infection, but Sarah saw to it that my feet always looked glamorous—even when the rest of me looked far from it.

One time, Sarah came over with a full wardrobe of pajamas and comfy clothes for me to lounge around in, because she wanted to make sure I felt pretty, even if I slept all day. The breadth and depth of her support was endless—cards, meals, house cleanings, rides to the doctor, and so much more.

∾ ∾ ∾

One afternoon at the end of June, after my third chemo, I was driving my new Beetle with the top down. Suddenly I noticed something flying around out of the corner of my eye.

I stopped at a red light, looked up in the rearview mirror and put my hand on the side of my head. With an ever-so-gentle pull, a tuft of long blond hair fell into the palm of my hand. A sinking feeling hit the pit of my stomach.

I really do have cancer. I really do. This is it. My hair is falling out.

My oncologist had prepared me for the loss of my hair. Even though he warned me that women have a difficult time losing their hair, I claimed it was not going to be a big deal, because all I really cared about was staying alive.

But that first handful of hair was a shocker.

Ignoring the reality of going bald, even temporarily, helped get me through the next couple of days. But one morning as I sat on my screened-in porch, pulling out gobs of hair, I gave in to the tears. My lap was covered with long, thick strands of blond hair.

I picked up the phone and called Sarah. "My hair is coming out. I don't know what to do. I don't want to lose my hair!"

"Don't worry, honey. Why don't you and Megan come over to my house, and we will do it together? We can have a party and give you a makeover."

Once again, sweet Sarah came through and made everything better. I sat in her bathroom, facing away from the mirror as Megan started to buzz my head with a pink electric razor. Then everyone took turns. All of us were giggling.

"Mom, you look pitiful," Megan said with amusement and pity. Yeah, just like that, she was a normal nine-year-old kid, completely real and saying it like it is.

"Oh, Meg, please tell me your mommy isn't ugly," I begged.

"Mommy, you are beautiful no matter what. I love you," she answered, reaching over to hug my neck.

Just then, I had a flashback to a few years earlier, when Megan and I were shaving Grammy's head. *What child should have to go through this twice? I have to live, God. Please don't take me, too.*

While I faced away from the mirror, Sarah got out her makeup and made me beautiful. I hadn't seen the damage yet, and my heart was racing. Sarah and Megan tried to keep me calm while they applied eye shadow, mascara, blush, and lipstick. They made me close my eyes for the big reveal.

As they spun me around, I slowly opened my eyes . . . and saw the new me.

My head was white; it was huge. I felt less than feminine—like a man with makeup on. I felt naked. I wanted to hide that hideous, bald dome.

Sarah obliged and quickly reached for a scarf.

As the weeks and months passed, every time I saw myself in the mirror, the reality of my new look, my new normal, looked back at me. It was difficult seeing myself stripped of the identity I thought was me. I never realized how much of my identity came from my outward appearance. It was quite unsettling to discover how superficial my thoughts were about who I really was. I no longer had anywhere to hide.

Sunday, June 28, 2009, 6:11 P.M.

So I took the plunge today and shaved my head! Megan helped, and it is very strange having no hair, but I know I will get used to it. I feel a little freaky being bald, but this is only one small piece of the climb to overcoming the cancer, so I feel pretty good about taking action myself and not waiting any longer. Please pray for me tonight that when I wake up tomorrow, I will not be too depressed about the hair thing. Thanks!

Peace, FROG—Linda

Although Megan was a real champ when it came to helping me when I was traumatized, sometimes it was clear that she was still just a scared little girl. This was especially true when the anniversary of her grandmother's death rolled around and I was still in the middle of my own battle to get well. Early on, she had plenty of anxiety about my being sick, even when she was trying to put on her brave face.

One night I was sound asleep, when I woke up with the strange feeling that someone was in the room. I opened my eyes to see my little girl standing beside me in the dark.

"Sweetie, what's wrong?" I whispered.

"Mommy, can you come lie down with me?"

I could hear the tears in her voice.

"Of course I can!"

"I'm really scared," she said as we walked upstairs to her bedroom.

With the bright moonlight shining through her bedroom window, I snuggled up in Meg's bed with her. Her head lay on my chest. I sang her a lullaby until she fell asleep. It reminded me of all the times I'd rocked her to sleep when she was just an infant.

Never in a million years would I have imagined that my little girl would experience so much heartache in her short life.

God, why does Meg have to go through this again? This is not fair.
Tears soaked my face.

Thursday, July 2, 2009, 4:55 A.M.

Yet I am confident I will see the LORD's goodness while I am here in the land of the living. Wait patiently for the LORD. Be brave and courageous. Yes, wait patiently for the LORD. (Ps. 27:13–14 NLT)

Yesterday was a very hard day for me physically. Please pray for my family and me to have patience right now. Meg still has much anxiety, and I really want Jesus to calm her sweet spirit. Yesterday was exactly two years since her Grandma (my sweet Judy) passed. I did not remind Meg about this, but I know deep down she was missing Grandma and confused about me. I know God is going to carry us every single day, and we will be everything he created us to be when this door closes. I only have one request and that is to earnestly pray for us today. I would really appreciate it. Thank you so much for all of your love.

Peace, FROG—Linda

~&~&~&

One Friday in mid-July, my good friend Debbie offered to take me to chemo. Debbie is like a momma to me, very loving and nurturing. When I'm with her, I feel a deep sense of peace. I feel safe when she's around. I was delighted to have her take me to chemo, because it meant Todd would get a much-needed break from all the doctor appointments. I had begun to see the toll it was taking on him to sit with me during those treatments. No matter how much he loved me, sitting in the infusion room was draining him.

When Debbie arrived at my house to pick me up, a strangely creative idea flooded into my mind.

"Debbie, I have this weird desire to paint a picture while I'm getting my treatment today," I said. "Do you mind helping me gather some of Megan's art supplies and a blank canvas to take with us?"

"Sure," Debbie agreed enthusiastically, "that sounds like fun."

The funny thing was that I can't even draw a straight line. But that day, I didn't care. I just wanted to create. I wanted to prove that cancer did not control me.

Hooked up to the chemo drip, I dipped my paintbrushes into color after color and dabbed haphazardly at the canvas. While I pretended to be the next Picasso, Debbie and I laughed so hard at my pitiful efforts that we almost cried. The nurses kept walking by to see what all the commotion was about.

Voila! My creation turned out to be a beautiful heart.

I had painted a vibrantly colorful heart with an array of fun colors. Interestingly, it had a black spot in the center and an abstract numeral five within the heart. I wouldn't notice the number five and its uncanny significance until many months later.

> **Friday, July 10, 2009, 9:26 P.M.**
>
> God is so, so good. Chemo went pretty good today.
> Thank you, Jesus! I painted a picture during chemo, and
> I will be sending copies of it out next week, so please
> email me your mailing address so everyone can see what
> God placed in my heart to paint. It is very special to
> me, and it shows how God has made this cancer thing a
> beautiful gift in my life. Thank you for your continued
> prayers, support, and love. I really appreciate each one
> of you.
>
> Love & joy, Peace FROG—Linda

The next day, I took a picture of my painting and ordered note cards online. I wanted to use them as thank-you notes. While ordering the cards, Romans 12:2 came to mind, and I referred to it on the back of the card.

Linda's New Heart

Don't copy the behavior and customs of this world, but let God transform you into a new person by changing the way you think. Then you will learn to know God's will for you, which is good and pleasing and perfect. (Rom. 12:2 NLT)

The black center represents the cancer in my body and the mass behind my heart. The beautiful rainbow of colors represents how God is using the cancer to change my life for him to bring New Life in my spirit so I can share Jesus' love with everyone I meet. Thank you, Jesus, for my cancer!

∾ ∾ ∾

In mid-September, we received great news. My treatments overall were going well, and my oncologist was very optimistic following the ninth round of chemotherapy. A PET scan showed that my treatments were working: the mass behind my heart had shrunk in half, and all of the cancer in my neck and lower abdomen was gone. I sent out an upbeat message through CaringBridge.

Friday, September 18, 2009, 1:22 P.M.
GREAT NEWS! Praise God!! He is sooo good to me! There is no cancer in my lower abdomen or in my neck. The mass behind my heart has shrunk from 10 x 5 cm to 3.6 x 4.6 cm. The doctor said the mass could possibly be scar tissue, but they will not know until I complete treatment and get another PET scan. I am getting chemo

as I type, and after this I will have three treatments left and will do radiation. I'm so grateful to God and to everyone who has been praying for my family and me all this time. All I can say with a huge smile is that God is so good to me!!! Thank you to all my friends and family for your love and support. I would not be in the position I'm in today if it weren't for you!

Love and Blessings, Linda (Fully Rely On God)

It was refreshing to be able to say that I was on the homestretch. One week later, everything changed.

CHAPTER SIX

Miracle

My bald head was lying heavy and still on a hospital bed. My cute black and tan convertible sat in the garage collecting dust.
I was fighting for my life in a completely unexpected way.

ON SEPTEMBER 28, MY FRIEND CATHERINE and I met for breakfast to celebrate the news that the treatment was doing its thing; however, we left that morning focused on something completely different.

There was no need for pretense with Catherine. I was able to say whatever was on my mind . . . and what was on my mind was that I was tired of being bald and fat, having gained about fifty pounds from the steroids that were supposed to help ward off side effects.

"Ya know, Catherine, I wish I could sleep through the rest of my treatments and then wake up with it all over!" I said, while I dug in to my omelet.

Catherine laughed and then abruptly looked at me with puzzled concern.

"What? Why are you looking at me so weird?" I asked.

"You don't look very well," Catherine said as she reached over the table and put her hand on my forehead and then my cheek. "I think you have a fever."

"Catherine, there is no way I have a fever. I'm fine."

"No," she said. "We are calling the oncologist right now."

Deep down, I knew I wasn't feeling well, but I'd just had chemo the week prior, and I wasn't in the mood for doctors.

Catherine called my oncologist right then and there and handed me the phone. The doctor didn't think I needed to be seen; instead he called in a prescription for antibiotics, which I picked up on the way home from breakfast. I got home and took my medicine and then spent the rest of the day in bed. That afternoon I rallied to pick up Megan from school.

I did have a slight fever, but I was convinced it really was nothing to worry about. We ate dinner and watched some television, and I went to bed a little earlier than normal.

The next morning, I could barely get out of bed. As soon as I opened my eyes, I felt the pounding in my head. I'd had chills all night long, feeling cold even with layers of covers over me. Somehow, I had slept a few hours off and on.

I told Todd to go to work, that I could take Megan to school. I really didn't want to bother him. My plan was to sleep all day until it was time to pick her up. As I dropped Megan off in the car-pool line, I reached over and gave her a kiss.

"I love you, sweet girl. Momma will see you after school."

"Okay, Mom, I love you to the moon and back!" she replied.

"I love you to the moon and back times a hundred."

"Mom, I love you to the moon and back times infinity!" Megan giggled, grabbed her lunch box and hopped out of the car.

For some reason, my heart ached as I watched her walk into the school. I had a feeling inside that I needed to stay with her and hug her for a few minutes. Sadness came over me—I wanted to get better so I could be her healthy momma again.

Maybe if I sleep all day again, I will have more energy tonight to do something special with her.

As I drove home, I grew weaker by the second. I felt like I had a horrible flu. My head was pounding, my body was aching. The chills were so bad that my teeth were chattering.

God, please tell me that this is not some sort of setback from the cancer.

I told myself I just had to get home and get back in bed. I just needed to sleep. I would feel better after I got some more sleep.

I was out the second my head hit the pillow.

Ring! Ring! Ring!

The sound of my cell phone seeped into my consciousness. I was so weak I could barely reach over to answer it. I knocked the thermometer off my nightstand.

"Hello," I whispered faintly.

"Hey there, how are you feeling today?"

Of course, it was Catherine checking in on me.

"Oh, I'm not feeling so well. I'm really tired. The last time I took my temperature it was 104 degrees," I answered.

"What? Linda, I'm coming over there right now and taking you straight to the oncologist. They will probably put you in the hospital," she barked.

"Catherine, I'm fine. I don't need to go to the doctor. I think if I can get some more rest, I'll be better by tomorrow," I said, knowing full well there was no way I was going to be able to stop her.

"Linda, I'm coming now. I will see you in fifteen minutes. We are going to the doctor." And she hung up the phone.

Ugh! I do not want to go to the doctor. She's being ridiculous. But I do feel like crap.

An hour later, as I sat on the exam table in the oncologist's office, my doctor spoke the feared words, "Linda, your white blood count is almost nonexistent. That means you have no immune system to fight off any infections. You are very sick. I'm going to admit you to the hospital."

"No, no, no," I pleaded, shaking my head as hot tears streamed down my face. "Please, I don't want to go to the hospital. Please don't make me go. Please. Please."

"Linda, this is just a little bump in the road," he assured me. "You will only be in the hospital for two days, just to get your immune system built back up, and then you will be home."

I heard Catherine in the background; she was on the phone telling my mother I was going to the hospital.

"Can I please just stop by my daughter's school and tell her Mommy's going to be gone for a few days?" I begged the doctor.

"No, Linda, you are way too sick to be around children. It would be extremely dangerous for you."

Deep down inside me I was frightened to death of some unknown hell I was getting ready to face. I felt like I wanted to escape, but I had nowhere to hide.

❧ ❧ ❧

Catherine drove me to the hospital that Tuesday afternoon. When we arrived, they offered me a wheelchair, but I refused it. I was determined to prove I was in control and that I was okay even though I could barely keep my head up.

As soon as I got to my assigned room, a nurse came in and swabbed my nose to test for the H1N1 swine flu, which was a pandemic that year. The test was negative, but I was put on Tamiflu as a precaution anyway.

Settling into my room, with nurses and IV drips all around me, I did what I do best: I took back control. I called and made arrangements for Megan to sleep over at Sarah's house that night. I made sure I had her car pool lined up for the next couple of days. Todd brought my laptop to me when he came to the hospital that afternoon, and I made a short video for Megan, telling her I would be home in a few days. I felt compelled to reassure her that I was going to be okay.

Ever since Todd's mom had passed away, Megan had kept a tight grip on me; it was a priority for me to keep life running smoothly and as normal as possible for her.

My fever never broke. Over the next two days, my breathing became shallower. As the weekend approached, I quickly began to go downhill.

I was put on oxygen, with the little nose thingamajigs, to help me get more air.

At times, I was unresponsive.

None of the medications were working.

Doctors and nurses constantly coming and going kept up a flurry of activity as my condition kept getting worse.

By Friday, I was barely able to breath on my own, even with the additional oxygen.

Hour by hour the doctors were not certain what was happening to me. They kept running tests and coming up with no conclusions.

Because I had tested negative for the flu, the doctors thought I might be having a reaction to one of the chemo drugs that carried the risk of permanent lung damage. A biopsy of my lung was needed to confirm.

The doctors told Todd and Mom there was a risk my body would not be able to handle the procedure. But at that point, they really had no choice but to move forward with it. They needed an answer quickly as to why I was not able to breathe.

I was prepped for the operating room. My family was reassured it would be a quick procedure.

Just as the doctors had cautioned, they were unable to perform the procedure. I almost went into cardiac arrest. They were unable to get a biopsy of my lung. They explained to Todd and Mom that my heart was working overtime trying to help me breathe.

That evening I was transferred to the intensive care unit for what was expected to be twenty-four hours. The doctors were puzzled and wanted to get me stabilized so they could run further tests.

During that twenty-four hours, I was in and out of consciousness but able to communicate with the doctors. They would ask me questions and explain what they were doing to me, and, apparently, I would respond. I have no recollection of any of it. Everyone was still confident the medical team would find the answers overnight as I was under observation.

The next morning, as Todd and Mom were standing at my bedside waiting for the doctor to arrive, they anticipated some much-needed answers as to what was going on with me. I was coherent, in and out of conversation with them.

The doctor showed up, his face and voice grave.

"Unfortunately, this is not what we expected," he said. "Linda has declined significantly overnight. She needs to be put into a medically induced coma."

"What? Why?" Todd was shocked.

"Sometimes comas are induced to allow the body time to heal with less stress," the doctor explained. "If you choose not to go that route, she will more than likely go into cardiac arrest."

He paused to let that sink in. "That means her heart will stop because it cannot keep up with the pressure it is under."

Todd heard the doctors' recommendation. He understood that the coma was my best option because it would allow me to rest and heal. But he was terrified at the prospect.

"How many days will she be in a coma?" he asked.

Of course, there was no definitive answer. Todd pressed them, and it became clear that there was no guarantee I would even come out of the coma.

What they did seem sure of, however, was that without the medically induced coma, I would eventually go into cardiac arrest. My heart would stop. And the chances were slim to none that, in my weakened state, I would survive such an ordeal.

The doctor demanded a decision. I was running out of time.

Todd and Mom were overwhelmed. They agreed to the coma.

Before she and Todd were ushered out of the room, Mom asked the doctors if they could pray.

My family and the doctors gathered around my bed holding hands. I had no conscious awareness of what was happening. Mom prayed.

"Lord, we are praying for a miracle for my baby girl. Thank you, Lord, for the entire medical staff. Guide them as they continue to treat her. I claim your healing in the name of Jesus. I love you, precious daughter, more than you will ever know. Thank you, Lord, that the blood of Jesus covers her. Amen."

∿ ∿ ∿

I was put on a ventilator. The coma was induced by medicines through IVs. I also was receiving massive amounts of steroids and many antibiotics.

An hour later, when Todd reentered my room, tubes and wires were everywhere. Machines were beeping. I was flat on my back, with the ventilator tube in my mouth and a feeding tube up my nose. My chest rose and fell with the rhythm of the vent.

I was comatose.

∿ ∿ ∿

My mom remained by my bedside 24/7. Night and day, friends and family came by for support. The beeping machines assured them I was still alive—beeping signified a steady heartbeat, and that was hopeful. Todd and Mom kept their eyes glued to the machines that monitored my oxygen and heart rate.

Catherine brought items from my home to decorate the room. She had Megan help her pick out special things around the house. Of course, the "Believe in Miracles!" sign was placed in the room. Mom added a photo of Megan and me hugging above my bed to show the doctors and nurses who they were fighting for—a young thirty-four-year-old mother and her daughter. My heart painting I had made a few months earlier was propped up against the window.

The words I painted across the bottom of the picture, Fully Rely On God, were a constant reminder that his presence was in the room.

My name was added to prayer lists in many churches. Even a church I no longer attended prayed for me daily.

The doctors made the decision to switch me over to an oscillator—a machine that basically breathes for patients who are in comas. In order to put me on the oscillator, they needed to also give me a paralytic drug made famous by Michael Jackson just a few months earlier. The King of Pop died from an overdose of this drug. The paralytic given through IV eliminated the chance of my body making any involuntary movements while I was on the machine and made it possible for my heart to slow down dramatically and my lungs to heal. During the time when I hadn't been able to take in enough oxygen, my heart had raced out of control, trying to keep me alive. If it kept going at that rate, the doctors feared it would soon give out.

Staying on the oscillator and the paralytic drug was extremely dangerous—any extended length of time might cause permanent damage to my organs or muscles.

After ten days in the coma my body still was not responding to the medicines. Even if—not *when*, but *if*—I pulled out of the coma, the doctors said chances were slim that I would walk or breathe again on my own.

There was not much hope. There was nothing else they could do.

The doctors said if my family believed in divine intervention, now was the time to ask for it. By their estimate, I had less than a 5 percent chance of living.

∾ ∾ ∾

When Catherine heard the devastating news that my chance of survival was so slim, she felt lost and powerless. My action-oriented friend immediately went to work doing the only thing she could think of that could possibly make a difference—planning a prayer gathering.

She wanted it to be at a place that I liked to go, so she chose a park where we often met each other to chat over coffee about our kids, husbands, and life.

The turnout of people at the prayer gathering represented every phase and stage of my life. People I had worked with, longtime friends, neighbors, pastors, and more. There they stood in the middle of a park with green balloons in hand. On each balloon was written the answer to one question: "What do you want to do with Linda when she wakes up?"

Most people wrote about the ordinary things of life, suddenly aware of how precious it can be just to have coffee together, go shopping, hug each other, and laugh together.

As these special people in my life released them, the balloons clustered in the sky, gradually taking on the shape of a butterfly.

People held hands. They lifted up heartfelt prayers. They declared, together, their belief that God could—and would—deliver a miracle.

∿ ∿ ∿

For more than three weeks, I existed on life support, hovering between life and death.

CHAPTER SEVEN

Lies

A CAPABLE, THIRTY-FOUR-YEAR-OLD WOMAN lying in a hospital bed, fighting for her life.

A twelve-year-old frightened teen lying in a hospital bed, wishing she had died.

A three-year-old little girl cuddling her teddy bear in bed, aching for her father's love.

From the age of three, feelings of unworthiness tormented me. I grew up feeling abandoned and ashamed, even though I had a loving mother who adored me. Self-destruction became my coping mechanism and my best friend.

My mother's life had a harsh beginning. Both of her parents were alcoholics. She learned to feel not good enough at a very young age, so early that she doesn't remember ever feeling any different. It was the same for me. It's almost as if feeling unworthy was in our blood; today, some might say that feeling unloved came with the territory of growing up around alcoholism.

Mom was only twenty-three years old when she left my biological father with two children, ages three (me) and five (my brother Rodney). She had no source of income, which spun her into a near breakdown as she tried to feed and keep a roof over the heads of her little ones. Momma had no choice but to seek help from the Department of Social Services. Willingly, she made arrangements for me and my brother to be placed in foster homes. She believed this was the best temporary answer for us until she could get her feet back on the ground.

Rodney and I were placed in two different homes. I do not have even the slightest memory of the home where I spent a few months. Mom told me that they were a loving Christian family who later became missionaries. She said the woman adored me so much that she hoped and prayed she would be able to adopt me. I have no doubt that I was in a nurturing home covered by ministering angels the entire time I was there.

My brother was in a Christian home, as well. The father was the pastor of a Methodist church, which my family joined years later.

Of course, a three-year-old can't understand the gut-wrenching choices adults can face when life deals them horrible blows. I couldn't understand what it was like for my mother to wake up every morning wondering if this was the day we would go hungry or have to go to bed without a roof over our heads. I couldn't understand the desperation that drove her to make the hardest choice a mother can make to be sure her children are safe. As a three-year-old, I couldn't help feeling confused. I was sent away from everyone and everything I knew. I believed it was my fault. There must have been something wrong with me. Surely I had caused my father to leave and my mother to send me away. This is what I grew up believing.

While Rodney and I were in foster care, Mom fell in love with a man who was young and, just like her, wanted nothing more than to have a family. He was ready and willing to help provide a stable environment for us. After Rodney and I came home from foster care, Mom married him and he became our "daddy." We never considered him to be a stepdad. He was our daddy, and we believed he loved us very much and worked hard to give us a traditional home life.

Sometimes that traditional home life meant we would go to church as a family. Most Sunday mornings, however, the church van would pick up my brother and me for Sunday school. Daddy often stayed home because he had been drinking too much the night before.

I grew up in that Sunday school singing "Jesus loves me this I know . . . ," but the words never soaked in to my heart. Church was simply something we had to do, kind of like going to school.

My only memorable church experience was one evening—most likely a Christmas Eve service. I vividly remember my mom starting to cry and walking to the altar to pray. Because I was so young, it frightened me to see Mom crying. I didn't understand what was happening at that moment. Over time I came to understand that my mom and my grandmother believed in and loved Jesus Christ with their whole hearts. *Their* faith was what I believed in more than Jesus.

Despite being reunited with my family after foster care, despite my Mom's faith, I carried scars. Scars that continued to impact me and my behavior.

I was a bad little girl who pitched fits.

From the time I returned to my mother until I was about school age, I threw outrageous tantrums. My outbursts meant blood, sweat, and tears. I pulled out fistfuls of hair and clawed my cheeks until they bled. I ripped the curtains from the windows in my bedroom and tore the pictures off the walls while kicking and screaming.

My new daddy was not around when these tantrums occurred. Maybe he was at work. Maybe he disappeared to avoid conflict and escape in the bottle. Mom couldn't handle me either. But she tried to find a solution to this difficult child who had returned to her from foster care. Sometimes she took me to our neighbor's house for help. Our neighbor would sit me up on the kitchen counter and lecture me, gripping my arm tightly and pointing her finger in my face. Her harsh tone of voice and the fierce expression on her face scared me enough that I would settle down quickly.

By the time I was six, I had outgrown my tantrums and turned into a pretty little princess. Mom put me in dance lessons and beauty pageants. She hoped it would give me self-confidence. I had tons of fun dancing in my pink leotard, tights, and tutu. I loved making new friends. And nothing was more exciting than getting all fixed up for beauty pageants. The beautiful gowns, hair, and makeup made me feel like I was in a fairy tale. Winning glamorous tiaras and stunning awards made the experience all that more enticing. I heard the love every time I won.

"Oh, what a pretty little girl."

"Isn't she adorable!"

"You did such a good job."

Of course, sometimes I didn't win. When the praise didn't come, I believed I was unlovable.

Between the dancing and the pageants, I fell in love with performing, and with being the center of attention and admired for being talented. It quickly became my identity. All the affirmations meant I was lovable. I lived for the applause and the praise because I equated those things with love.

Every time I won a pageant I would cry as they crowned me the new reigning queen. After all the hard work and dedication, the tears were my expression of joy. I loved doing pageants. Mom was right; it did help me gain confidence.

One evening after winning many awards and being crowned best overall, which was a big accomplishment, my daddy made a comment that made me very sad and confused. "Why do you cry when you win? You look silly being so emotional."

This judgment broke my heart.

A daddy is supposed to be proud of his little girl and her accomplishments, but that was not my relationship with this stepfather who was the only father I could recall. I had learned to be on guard around him, to be protective of myself, because his judgments were often harsh and his words often angry, although he was never violent. He often belittled my successes and, as I reached adolescence, made me feel very uncomfortable with my femininity.

I did not say a word to anybody about it, but I begin to feel loads of shame. Doing well felt wrong. I was no longer lovable because of my achievements.

The spotlight began to feel degrading. I was uncertain where or how to find my self-worth.

❧ ❧ ❧

School didn't become a source of approval either.

In elementary school, I was a chatterbox. Just about every report card read, "Linda talks too much in class." In citizenship, I'd often get a big fat U for unsatisfactory. Actually, I got a lot of those Us. Acting out created negative attention, and at that point any attention felt right. I became accustomed to rejection and failure.

This was when the lies running through my head began to take control of me. The lies in my mind told me I was not valuable, that no one could really love me, that I did not deserve the good things in life.

The feelings of inadequacy—of being unlovable and unworthy—began to grow, especially when I was around authority figures in my life. I felt I never measured up and was always a disappointment. I decided early on in school that I was not smart enough, so I stopped trying. If I was not perfect, then I was useless.

One saving grace for my brother and me during our childhood was our grandmother. We loved her cooking, and we loved staying over at her house on Friday nights. We felt safe with our grandmother because at our house, Daddy would come home drunk most Friday nights and start yelling and screaming.

As far as church, I never understood it as a child. It was a place where I belonged, which meant a lot to a little girl who felt left behind. However, nothing that happened to me in church helped me see how God fit into my own life. Church was just Christmas plays, hymns, and memorizing a few Bible verses. Isn't that the case for many kids?

I was never able to connect the dots between what I learned in church and how it could change the way I lived my life. I saw my mother get saved and knew she "believed," but I don't remember fully understanding what that meant. I knew it meant she wouldn't go to hell. Being saved was a ticket to heaven.

I was simply too young to understand anything as profound as living for Christ, or accepting myself as a much-loved daughter of God. It certainly never would have occurred to me to pray for help.

With little to interrupt the unhappy direction of my life, by the time I was in third grade I became the troublemaker who made every teacher cringe. For me, school was only a place to socialize. I had no desire to learn.

By the fifth grade, I began to struggle with my appearance. Most girls, as adolescents and preadolescents, become obsessed with how they look, especially these days. I took my obsession to a whole different level. If every hair wasn't in place, I could become sick at my stomach. I sneaked into the girls' bathroom every chance I could to check myself in the mirror and make sure I looked as close to perfection as possible. I rarely heard anything that was said in class; I was too focused on how soon I could get away and check myself in the mirror.

No one knew what was going on inside my head until it almost was too late.

One September afternoon when I was twelve, while on the way home from the mall, I announced to Mom that I wanted to cut my long blond hair. My best friend had short hair and, being an adolescent with the need to fit in, I wanted short hair, too.

"We're not getting your hair cut," Mom said firmly. "You know that's not a good idea with your pageants and your dancing."

"I don't care about that!" I insisted adamantly. "Please, Mom!"

She shook her head and gave me the look that said her mind was made up. "Linda, I know you. You'll hate it, and there won't be a thing you can do about it and you'll just make yourself crazy fretting over it. We're not going through that."

"But, Mom!"

"I'm not changing my mind on this, young lady."

The argument turned into an epic battle. Mom and I both said ugly things to each other.

By the time I got home, I had worked myself into a frenzy. As soon as I walked through the front door, I headed straight to the medicine cabinet.

The ugly things Mom and I had said to each other weren't the only things spinning around in my head. There were other lies. The lies that lived in my head day in and day out. At the age of twelve, I was already beaten down and exhausted from listening to them. From believing them.

You're stupid and you're ugly.

I stared in the mirror at my tear-streaked face and knew without a doubt this was true.

Everybody hates you, because you suck.

The things my mom and I had said in anger made it so much easier to believe that.

Nobody cares if you live or die.

The lies filled me up and became my truth.

You should just end the pain now, and you won't have to put up with all of this.

One by one, lie by lie, I swallowed an entire bottle of prescription pills.

In my bedroom, with no water, I used the saliva in my mouth to get the pills down my dry throat. I started to panic. *God, what have I done?*

I staggered out into the living room and stood in front of my mom. Mom could tell that I was not right. My eyes were glazed over.

At first she thought the problem must have been that I had stayed up late at my friend's house the night before. After a few minutes of trying to talk with me, she realized something was really wrong.

She started screaming, "What have you done? Linda, did you take something?"

I would not answer her.

Frantic, she looked through my room and found the empty bottle of pills and rushed me to the hospital to have my stomach pumped.

~ ~ ~

Being locked in the hospital psychiatric unit for a week-long observation did not help my self-esteem issues at all.

I came into the hospital believing completely that I was screwed up and being in the psych ward confirmed the worst to me: I was officially a crazy lunatic.

I had been depressed for a long time, yet somehow I'd managed to hide it from everyone around me. My friends and family were in total shock that I had tried to commit suicide. No one saw it coming.

When Daddy came into my hospital room the night I was admitted, what I really wanted to hear—what I needed to hear— was, "I love you. Thank God, you are alive!" Instead, he sat there looking at me with disgust on his face. He was humiliated and disappointed in me.

Shaking his head, he said to the doctor, "She just did this for attention."

His words cut me like a knife. Shame suffocated me. Immense self-hatred lured my soul. All those lies that had paved the way for this hospitalization in the first place came flooding back into my head and my heart.

I had swallowed those pills to avoid ever feeling this way again. But the pills had not solved the problem.

When I was alone again, I started hitting myself, clawing my face and gripping my hair. It was like I was three again. All the confused self-loathing that little girl felt had never been dealt with. Applause and trophies had only masked the feelings that went so very deep.

More than ever I wanted to die. I was angry that my attempt had failed.

I'll show you what getting attention looks like, I thought. *Just wait and see when I get out of this hospital. I'll be smarter the next time, and it will work.*

Sitting in the psych unit for a week gave me plenty of time to drown in my shame and humiliation, and to build my rage. Talking to the counselor was frustrating because I was too embarrassed to admit the crazy thoughts I had about myself. I was afraid I would be locked up for life if anyone knew how much I hated myself. It helped to talk about my daddy's drinking and our strained relationship. But I was never able to get honest enough to root out the problems that went so deep.

As a little girl, I wanted nothing more in the world than to have a daddy who adored me and who assured me that I was a priceless treasure. All I'd ever desired was a daddy's love—acceptance, security, and worthiness. But that night sitting in my hospital bed, I felt the sting of unworthiness in every inch of my being as he uttered those ugly words, "She just did this for attention."

After my daddy made that comment, I was wrecked. I really wasn't good enough to love, even by my second dad.

✌ ✌ ✌

After I left the hospital, Mom took me for the haircut, which I ended up hating.

Back at school, I tried to get back to a sense of normalcy, which, at the age of twelve, included the drama of liking boys. A couple of days after leaving the hospital, I asked my best friend to find out if a boy I liked also liked me. I found a way to stand nearby so I could eavesdrop on the conversation.

She never really got around to asking the all-important question. As soon as she brought up my name, the boy I was crushing on said, "You're not going to still be friends with that suicidal maniac, are you?"

That was it. I was a freak. What everyone was saying about me proved it.

His words destroyed me. They joined the chorus of taunts in my head, telling me I wasn't lovable. Wasn't even likable. Telling me I was not worthy.

In my very small elementary school, the word "privacy" apparently did not exist. Believing, I suppose, that my experience would open up a conversation about suicide—maybe even believing it would encourage my classmates to be supportive when I returned to school, the sixth-grade teachers shared with their classes that I had tried to take my life.

The conversation opened up all right, but it was not supportive.

✌ ✌ ✌

My entry into middle school was shaky. Besides the story of my attempted suicide following me into my new school, my mom and dad divorced about that time. I was sad and relieved all at the same time.

Mom remarried a wonderful man, Tommy. Tommy never tried to be a father to me, even though I consider him as my father today. He was more like a friend and mentor. He believed in me. He was proud of me as he sat through many very long dance recitals. He encouraged me in my education. For the first time in my short life, I had a healthy relationship with a male authority figure.

This new experience was freeing, and I slowly began to feel more comfortable in my own skin. I was grateful. But I was still a teenager—a far from perfect teenager.

Between sneaking out at night, drinking, and even getting arrested for shoplifting, I gave my mom and Tommy a pretty fair share of teenage craziness.

But my teenage years were also graced with the most amazing God-given gift—a person who became my best friend . . . and more. God put the perfect young man in my life.

∾ ∾ ∾

I met Todd Kuhar when I was fourteen years old.

Todd was a soccer player and a heavy metal fanatic. He wore skin-tight black jeans, black T-shirts, and had a smile that made me melt. I was attracted to his sense of humor, charm, and adorable dimples. I thought he was a little on the wild side but quickly learned that wasn't the case. He was sensitive to my needs and treated me with respect. He had a *Leave It to Beaver* type of family.

Another big plus—Todd's mother, Judy, loved me like I was her very own daughter right from the start.

I loved spending time at Todd's house because of the love and kindness Judy showered on me. Judy truly was Jesus in action during our early years together. I would tell her she was my "Jesus," and she would laugh and say she was far from that. She was humble, selfless, and the best listener. She was always fully engaged in our conversations.

Spending so much time with the Kuhars during my teen years saved me, I believe, from becoming completely out-of-control with no prayer of return.

Todd wasn't a big churchgoer in those days. In fact, our beliefs almost came between us right before we married. We were meeting with the pastor a few days before our wedding, and I told Todd he had to be saved before we got married. I ended up walking out on that meeting two days before the wedding because I wasn't sure whether Todd had been saved.

The truth is, I wasn't always convinced of my own salvation status.

Not long after Todd and I starting dating at fourteen, a childhood friend invited me to attend a concert by the Christian band New Song. Tracy had fallen passionately in love with Jesus and felt led by the Lord to invite me to attend the concert with her. I always loved spending time with her and was thrilled to get together for a girl's weekend.

This was my very first concert. I was surprised that a Christian concert could be so exciting. The loud music and flashing lights were so different from the Christian music I'd heard in the tiny country Methodist church I grew up in.

At the end of the concert, there was an altar call. I felt a tug in my soul to go forward. I didn't go up at first. But as I stood there watching others go forward, I was overtaken by emotion and went up front to accept Jesus Christ as my Savior.

People up front were there to pray with me. I wept as I asked Jesus to come into my heart. I knew he was what I needed to get my life in order. But even while I listened to the prayers for me, even as I wept, I started to have my doubts.

I shouldn't do this, I began to tell myself. *I shouldn't do this.*

Looking back, I can see clearly that they weren't doubts about my belief. I believed deeply that Jesus was there for me. What I doubted was my own ability to be a "good enough" Christian.

What if I couldn't follow all the rules I believed came with being a Christian? What if being a Christian meant being weird in the eyes of my teenaged friends?

Does this mean I have to give up all the things I like to do? I found myself wondering as I turned around and headed back to my seat. *The things I know I'm not supposed to do, but do anyway? Like going to parties and drinking. I still want to have fun. I'm just not too sure if this is for me—if I can do it.*

Even on the night I accepted Jesus, the voices that lied to me were awake and active.

Tracy was so excited for me, and I was afraid to tell her I was already questioning everything. That very night I resolved that there was no way I was going to give up having fun or become a prudish church girl.

The war raged inside my mind that night and for some time to come. I was bombarded with doubts and fears. I resigned myself to the fact that I believed in Jesus, but that was it. I was not going to try to change my life. And I never talked to anyone about my doubts. I just carried the doubts—and the feelings of being unworthy that were now growing in me even faster—hidden within me.

The main thing, I thought at the time, was that I had my ticket to heaven.

The truth is, I was in a spiritual coma for a long time. It would take a physical coma to fully reveal to me how to have a relationship with Jesus.

CHAPTER EIGHT

Trapped

FOR THE THREE AND A HALF WEEKS I was on life support, my hospital room was a revolving door.

While my life hung by a thread, family and friends were in and out, in and out. The waiting room was filled with tears and prayers that God would perform a miracle.

While they spent most of their time appealing to heaven, my only real recollection was being in my own personal version of hell.

My brother, Rodney, and his wife came. Even my birth father and his new family came. Friends from my neighborhood and my church came to pray for me and keep me company, even though no one had any idea whether I was aware of their presence or not.

The real rock, of course, was Mom. She sat by my swollen, helpless body for almost a month, ignoring the tubes and machines and focusing instead on the presence of the Holy Spirit she felt hovering over me, protecting and healing me. Although she barely ate and slept only from complete and utter exhaustion, she prayed long and hard for that healing, both for the sake of my daughter and for the sake of the many lives that could be touched by the story of my healing.

She was unwilling to leave anything to chance. She was going to fight for me—with the hospital and the doctors, certainly, and even, if necessary, with God.

Not everyone came to the hospital in those early days with their minds set on healing. After hearing that the doctors had given me a less than 5 percent chance of surviving, my Aunt Sharon came to Charlotte packed for a funeral. She knew the pain of losing a child—Sharon had lost two sons—and begged God not to take me. Although she prayed for healing, she also prayed that I would not suffer.

Nevertheless, when she reached the hospital and saw the doctor, she told him, "You do not know this child. She is a true fighter. I know God is with her and on her side and that she still has so much to do on this earth."

Then she turned to me, held my hand, and kept saying, "We're here with you, Linda. You need to fight. Keep fighting."

As she sat with me, as scared as everyone was, she felt the presence of death as well as God's presence. Deep down, she felt that, with God's grace, I would make it.

My friend Catherine, on the other hand, sat by my side feeling that the song of our friendship had been silenced.

In the back of her mind was the number the doctors had given my family: 5. A 5 percent chance of survival.

When Catherine got that news, she began to prepare for the worst, even asking the Lord to take me home quickly so everyone could grieve. She recalls, "My religious cloak quickly became transparent, showing underneath the core of a person more selfish than selfless. It just hurt too badly. Linda was like a sister to me. She was my strength and my rock. I could not bear the pain of losing her, but more than that, I could not bear sitting in the pain long enough to have faith move a mountain that seemed way too big to move."

She gave up and expected others to do the same. They didn't.

She caught Todd walking out of the intensive care unit one night and asked him what he was going to do, how he was going to cope. He looked at her as if she had three heads. Clearly surprised at her question, he said, "I'm not going to do anything but wait until she wakes up."

Todd's undaunted faith took her aback. Todd wasn't "churchy," wasn't one to wear his faith on his sleeve, go to Bible study, or talk openly about God. Why, Catherine wondered, wasn't he being practical? He knew the numbers. For goodness sake, he dealt in numbers for work!

Five percent. Hadn't he heard those words? Five percent!

As Catherine walked to her car that night, she realized that if ever there was a time to have faith, it was right then. If ever there was a time to trust that God could do something, move something, heal something, it was then.

The tiniest seed of something was planted in her that night. She picked up the phone and began calling anyone and everyone. We need to pray, she told them. We need to have faith.

Her mustard seed joined theirs and together they began to ask God for a miracle.

✧ ✧ ✧

One of my visitors was my stepdad Tommy's sister, Tammy. She drove four hundred and fifty miles to visit me, specifically to let me know that God was not finished with me.

Like everyone who visited me, Tammy had to put on hospital scrubs and gloves to keep from bringing in any kind of infection. I was too weak, physically, to fight off a serious infection.

Aunt Tammy was shocked at what she saw—my bloated body, my bald head, a face she barely recognized as her vibrant, happy, young niece, breathing only with the assistance of a respirator that seemed as loud to her as a lawn mower on Sunday morning.

When she walked into the room, she could feel death looming.

Yet somehow, she knew I was still in there, still fighting.

Stepping up to the bed, she nevertheless decided to speak up to the niece she hoped and prayed was in there somewhere.

"Linda, it's Aunt Tammy!" she called out, almost yelling—maybe to be heard over the sound of the breathing machine or maybe to get through to whatever dark place my spirit had gone. "Linda, you have got to come out of this. You are not done here yet!"

Although I was unresponsive, Tammy felt a sweet spirit come over the room, a spirit that was stronger than the death she had felt looming there. Somehow, Tammy knew everything was going to be okay.

Janet, Todd's aunt and Judy's sister, came to visit me as well. Our relationship had always centered on home design and fashion.

After losing her sister to cancer, Janet found the hospital scene was all too familiar. She leaned over my bed and whispered, "I promise when you wake up I'll take you shopping and buy you a Louis Vuitton."

"What did you tell her?" Todd asked.

"I told her I will buy her a purse when she wakes up!"

Even surrounded by the possibility of death, they enjoyed a good laugh.

The day after Janet's visit, I was transferred to a less intense breathing machine. The intention was to start bringing me out of the coma.

Within minutes, I became agitated, experienced convulsions, and dislodged the tubes. When my eyes opened, Todd saw what he could only describe as the eyes of a crazy woman. He thought I looked frightened and ready to flee—if only I had been able to.

I had to be sedated.

The baby steps to bring me back had begun.

∿ ∿ ∿

People ask me all the time what it was like being in a coma.

They want to know if I had some out-of-body heavenly experience. I think, deep in their hearts, they are hoping the answer is yes.

The answer is no. Not for me.

My coma was in no way heavenly. My only real recollection is feeling trapped and suffocating. Constantly panicking. Fighting to get out of my body. It was a scary, torturous hell. There was no sense of time. No hope. No light. And no sense that anything was ever going to change.

The coma became my sense of eternity.

Some people ask if I think I went to hell. Again, the answer is no.

I do, however, believe I was in the middle of a spiritual battle. A battle I do not try to understand. I did not see angels or demons. But I was in a constant state of pure panic.

If that sounds like hell to you, it sure felt that way to me.

Even as I type these words, I have to remind myself to breathe because my body slips into a state of shock when I think about my coma.

Even though I cannot explain what was happening to me during those three and a half weeks on life support, I know a spiritual transformation was happening within me and throughout my world.

∾ ∾ ∾

The hour will come when each of us will die. We all know that, although most of us try like crazy to forget it, deny it, or ignore it.

The why, when, and how people die may never make sense to us here on earth. But no matter the way or the time we die, I believe God has a plan and purpose for every single life. One is not greater than the other. But every life is here for a divine purpose and time.

God has our days numbered.

My number did not come up in the year 2009.

CHAPTER NINE

Awake

SLIVERS OF LIGHT.

No more dark.

Sounds.

"You're a miracle."

Voices?

"You almost died."

It's too bright. The light is hurting my eyes.

I'm cold. It's heavy. I'm not trapped anymore.

My mother was talking to me. She was next to me.

But where am I?

"You're going to be okay, sweetie," she said. "Don't worry, you're going to be okay."

I felt her hand on mine. I wanted to move. *Why can't I lift my hand? Why can't I move my head?*

As I awoke from the coma, my eyes frantically scanned the room.

What's happening?

Cancer. I have cancer.

Was I in a car accident?

I want to talk. Why can't I talk? I'm in a bed.

My body is heavy. Why is it so heavy? I can't move.

I try to look around the room.

Where's Todd? Where's Megan?

～◈～◈～◈～

On October 19, I started coming out of the medically induced coma.

It took several days of blinking and small facial movements happening off and on for me to fully wake up.

As I fell in and out of awareness of my surroundings, my family kept steadily talking to me and encouraging me to wake up. I appeared to be depressed, and I had a blank look in my eyes.

On October 22, I was moved from ICU to the step-down unit. This was tremendous progress. I was finally stable but required monitoring because I had the potential of becoming unstable again.

I was off the oscillator machine that did all the breathing for me and now on the ventilator that helped me breathe. When I fully regained consciousness, I realized tubes were coming out of every orifice of my body—including orifices that had never existed before my health crisis. A feeding tube ran up my nose, down the back of my throat and into my stomach. I felt like I was constantly gagging. There was also something wrapped around my neck. Very cold air was coming out of my throat. It was the trach—the tube that had been inserted during my tracheotomy to facilitate breathing. I had an IV they had inserted for antibiotics, fluids, and pain medications to be administered. A PICC line—a peripherally inserted central catheter—had been placed in my upper left arm for continued blood sampling. Wires attached all over my torso monitored my heart activity. Attached to my left middle finger was an oxygen monitor. They used the port for my chemo in my upper left chest to administer drugs as well.

When I tried to speak, nothing came out of my mouth. Silence. No words. I panicked.

Why can't I talk? What's happening? Did someone hurt me?

Mom could tell by the look in my eyes that I was distraught and wanted to talk to her. I kept mouthing words, but she was unable to understand what I was trying to say.

"What if I get you a pen and some paper to write with?" she asked me.

I blinked my eyes to indicate a panicked yes.

She searched the room and quickly found paper and pen.

"Here, honey, try this."

Mom put the pen in my hand, but I had no grip. The pen fell from my limp fingers.

Terror set in.

What has happened to me? I can't even hold a pen!

My heart started racing.

Why don't my fingers work? Why can't I move? Am I paralyzed?

Of course, everyone had been telling me in the most reassuring way what had happened, telling me gently that I was on the road to recovery following the induced coma. But I was unable to understand or retain information.

I started crying. Again, no sounds were coming out of me. I had no voice. Only tears leaking from the sides of my eyes and down my cheeks.

I just want to have cancer. What happened to me? Can I please just have cancer? I don't want to be an invalid.

Mom held my hand tightly. "I know you're scared. I'm right here. I promise you are going to be okay."

When that didn't dry my tears, Mom tried again to tell me the story of the last month. "Do you know what happened to you, sweetie?"

I tried to mouth the word no.

"You got really sick and almost died," she said softly. "The doctors put you in a coma to save your life. But that's all over now. You're back."

I still couldn't fully grasp what had happened to me.

"You had your thirty-fifth birthday while you were asleep."

Tears poured down my face. Inside, I was freaking out. My body felt like a dead weight, heavy, as if I were pushing with all my strength against people who were holding me down against my will.

I want to get out of this bed! Will I ever be able to move again? Both angry and afraid, I thought my life was over. *Am I going to be bedridden forever?*

If this is my life, I do not want to live.

My mom finally called in the nurse to give me some medication to calm me down.

"Are you in pain?" The nurse asked. "If you are, blink your eyes for me one time."

I had too much medication in me to feel anything physically. Yet even in the fog of confusion I was in, I knew instinctively that if I was in pain, I would be given something that would likely knock me out. And right at the moment, all I wanted was to escape the reality I had awakened to.

I blinked.

The nurse hesitated. "How much pain? I'm going to hold up some fingers. One finger means just a little bit of pain and ten means the worst pain you've ever felt. Understand?"

I blinked again.

"You let me know when I reach the level of pain you're in right now."

I ignored her fingers going up one at a time until she was holding up eight fingers.

Mom looked alarmed. The nurse just nodded and went away. When she returned, she had medication.

As soon as the medication traveled through the IV tube and into my veins, I fell fast asleep.

After so long in a coma, it might seem that the last thing a person would want was more oblivion, that they might welcome being alert to the world. But sleep was oblivion. After the emotional and mental anguish of feeling trapped in the coma, sleep was blessed relief.

This cycle of waking up and wanting nothing more than to go back to sleep went on for another three days.

I would wake up and, thinking I was completely paralyzed and unable to communicate, I would panic. Then a nurse would administer more Dilaudid, a heavy-duty pain reliever. I wasn't in pain, but I quickly figured out that if I nodded to indicate that I was, then I would receive the meds and I could go back to sleep.

Escaping my body—this body trapped in the bed—was my goal.

One time when I woke up, I saw my friend Catherine tearfully gazing into my eyes.

"I thought I'd never see those bright-blue eyes again," she said. "You are a miracle, Linda! You are an absolute miracle! Thank you, God!"

That's the first time I remember someone using that word to describe me and my situation. It would not be the last. Person after person who came to see me said the same thing.

"You're a miracle."

"God has some great big plans for your life, Linda! He has done a miracle."

I didn't believe them. I was confused. I had no idea if I would regain the ability to move or breathe again on my own. I was terrified that I'd turned into a vegetable. The new reality was incomprehensible.

And I was furious!

∿ ∿ ∿

Whenever I was awake, my mind continued to race.

Where is my Megan? Oh my goodness, how long has it been since she's seen me?

I wanted to see my daughter but had no way of asking anyone about her or demanding that someone bring her so I could see her.

And as the time seemed to drag on with no change in my condition, I found myself wondering in confusion, *How long have I been here? Days? Weeks? Months? Years?*

What if my little girl was all grown up? What if I had missed all of it?

Talk about panic. That one thought created more panic and anxiety than anything else. I think I could have taken the news that I would never walk again more easily than I could have taken hearing that I had missed my little girl growing up and becoming a young woman. But I could do nothing, absolutely nothing, to ask for reassurance at that point.

About five days after waking up from the coma, Todd was in the room with me one morning when the doctor came around to do his routine check. To my surprise, the doctor gave me the best news I'd heard yet. I was gaining a little more strength, and my breathing was improved just enough for a speaking valve to be placed briefly on my trach. This allowed my voice to come through, so that I could speak more easily. I was only able to use the device for short periods of time, but I was ecstatic! Finally, I could ask the questions that had been wracking my brain.

"How long was I in a coma?"

"You were in a coma for almost a month," said my doctor.

Thank God! That meant there was still time to be part of my daughter's life. I gave myself a moment to collect myself. I had too many questions to let myself cry at this point.

"Do I still have cancer?"

"Well, you were unable to complete your chemotherapy treatments. We will need to run further tests to find out where things stand."

I knew doctors well enough at this point to know an evasive, half answer when I heard one.

"Then I can finish the chemo?"

"At this point in time, given all that your body has been through, you will not be able to take any more chemo."

That sounded suspiciously like a veiled death sentence to me. "How will I get rid of the cancer if I cannot take chemo?"

"Let's not get ahead of ourselves. We need to get you out of the hospital first before we worry about the cancer."

I reminded myself that at least I was alive right now.

I turned to Todd. "How's Megan? Does she know what happened to me? She must be so scared."

"Megan came to see you when you were in the coma . . . when the doctors thought . . ." Todd hesitated. ". . . when they thought you were not going to make it. She has been such a trooper. You would be so proud of how strong and brave she's been the whole time."

Todd, I learned, had done a lot of negotiating with the hospital administrator to allow Megan to see me in ICU, possibly for the last time. Because of the H1N1 (swine flu pandemic) in 2009, hospitals did not allow children to visit. Todd had taken pictures of me lying in the bed on life support, so he could prepare Megan for what I looked like. He said she was so happy to hold my hand and kiss my cheek when she came to visit me.

My poor baby girl! She needs me. I've got to get home.

The fight was on. I was determined to get out of the hospital. Fast! Nothing was going to stop me. My mothering instincts kicked in, and my focus was to get home to Meg immediately.

A colorful painting hung on the wall by my bed. Megan and my mom had painted it together. A house, trees, blue sky, a sun, birds, and a small dog in the grass. This painting was even more motivation. Every time I looked at it, I thought about my little girl waiting and wondering when her momma was coming home.

My mind was made up. I was going to be 100 percent whole again for my family.

As determined as I was, the doctors and nurses weren't so certain. While I'd been in the coma, they had cautioned my family that recovery could take a long time in a rehab facility, or that I might end up in long-term care. The emphasis was not on *when* I would be home, but *if* I would make it home at all.

"Linda, it might be months before you are able to breathe on your own off the vent," my pulmonologist explained to me when I asserted my plan to get out of bed. "Many patients coming off an oscillator machine and paralytic drugs do not experience a full recovery."

Never recover? Oh, hell no! I am getting out of this bed today!

A few hours later, when I was alone in my room, I tried to sit up. Even though I had zero use of my muscles (they had completely atrophied), somehow I managed to scoot myself to the edge of the bed. My legs hung down and became dead weight over the side. I couldn't move my arms.

My plan was to escape.

My irrational, but powerful, mind had willed me to sit up, get out of this bed, and make my getaway. So I sat there surprised and unmoving like a rag doll. I began to realize that realistically my next move might actually be figuring out how in the world I was going to lie back down.

Alarms started blaring, and two nurses ran into my room. They were aggravated with me.

I realized I had a very long way to go.

Mom later told me that the young girl in her early twenties in the room next to mine in ICU, who had been diagnosed with H1N1, eventually went into a nursing home after coming off the oscillator. This machine had the potential to cause permanent damage to organs and muscles.

Todd planned to bring Meg for a visit now that I was out of ICU. I hadn't seen her in over a month and I was eager to see her. But I was afraid for my little girl to see me so helpless, not realizing the full extent of what she had already witnessed while I was on life support.

As Meg entered my room, I started to cry. She ran to my bed and gently laid her little head on my lap. I stroked her pretty hair and looked at her little fingertips and the soft, pink polish she liked to use. She looked up at me, and I mouthed, "I love you. Momma's going to be okay."

After we'd cuddled for a bit, she touched my hands and said, "Mommy, your Shrek hands are all gone."

My hands had been so swollen with fluids when she saw me while I was comatose that Meg had told her dad that I had huge, puffy hands like the animated movie character Shrek. My hands were not quite back to normal, but they were getting there. I smiled at her and she giggled. She didn't seem freaked out by all my tubes or my swollen face. I knew she must be working hard to appear strong.

The hour with her went by too quickly. Meg told me all about painting with Nana. And about a scrapbook she made of her and me with Nana's friend Angela, who had come from Alabama to help my mom.

It soothed me and gave me hope to be with Meg and Todd again. But when they walked out the door to go home, it felt like my heart was being ripped out of my chest. I had to get home. I had to get healthy.

❧ ❧ ❧

Afraid and furious at the state I was in, I could be a very defiant patient, especially at night, when I was alone and felt so helpless. Then, even though I was on heavy narcotics, I had a lot of fight in me and my true colors came out.

My rebelliousness could be a living nightmare for the nursing staff. I can see that more clearly now, although at the time I could only see it through my perspective of fear and my impatience for life to get back to normal.

Halloween night became a real-life horror show for me.

Todd had taken Megan trick-or-treating, and I was alone in my hospital room. I had gained some strength but still didn't always think clearly. But I was strong enough, at last, to pull out the annoying feeding tube that ran down the back of my throat. It made me gag horribly.

When I managed that little bit of rebellion, the alarm sounded. Nurses rushed in to see what was wrong. They were quite perturbed to realize what I'd done. And I was not cooperative when they tried to undo it. They finally had to pin me down to reinsert the feeding tube. It was painful, and I felt like I was going to throw up.

Because I was now even more angry and defiant, they felt they had no choice but to strap my hands to the bed to make sure I wouldn't cause any more trouble or do myself any harm.

Then they turned off the light and left my room.

After all I'd been through, I felt like a kid being punished. It was humiliating. And I was in no emotional state to understand that they were doing what they thought they had to do to keep me from hurting myself.

The humiliation turned out to be the least of what I ended up feeling that night.

My TV had been left on, and black-and-white horror movies played all night in recognition of Halloween. Because my hands were tied down, I could not reach the remote control to turn it off or to press the nurse call button. I wanted to yell for help, but I still had no voice from the tracheotomy.

I lay there in the dark all night, with only the glare of the TV screen and light from the hallway. People passed by in the hallway throughout the night, but I didn't see a nurse the rest of the night. Unable to sleep, I lay there in sheer panic. I began to sweat profusely. I started having trouble breathing because my trach had not been suctioned since early in the evening. The bed sheets were on the floor where I had kicked them during the night, trying to free myself or get someone's attention. My right foot was banging against the bedrail.

Just after dawn the next morning, my mother arrived and saw the state I was in. "Oh, my goodness! What happened to you, honey?"

Relieved but still in a state of panic, I mouthed the words, "They were mean to me!"

Mom flew out the door and headed straight to the nurses' station.

Today, I realize that being helpless and immobile in the hospital is a prescription for frustration for everyone—patients, family, and medical staff. Add to that my natural inclination to rebel and to panic, and it's easy to understand how desperate I was to get out.

And I'm sure the members of the hospital staff were equally relieved when I finally made my escape.

∾ ∾ ∾

My determination paid off.

My recovery—relearning how to stand, walk, climb stairs, and the basics of taking care of myself—should have taken months.

It took only about two weeks.

At every step, the doctors and nurses kept saying my speedy recovery was a miracle. Every visit, every checkup, that's what I heard. "This is a miracle."

At that point, all the talk of miracles went right over my head. My focus wasn't on God or Scriptures or prayer. All I knew was that I wanted to get out of the hospital immediately. I wanted to go home to Megan and Todd. I felt sometimes as if I knew my child was at home, drowning, and I was determined to jump in and save her. That's how urgent recovering felt to me.

I was moved from the step-down unit to a regular room. I demanded my clothes and when the doctor came in the next day, I was fully dressed.

"What are you doing?" my doctor asked when he made his rounds.

"Going home," I whispered hoarsely.

The doctor laughed. "You're not going anywhere, miss."

I'm sure I gave him my best defiant look.

"Mrs. Kuhar, you have a lot of ground to make up," he said gently but firmly. "You'll be in rehab for months. When you leave here, you may need to be in a long-term care facility. There are no guarantees."

He didn't know me. I decided that instead of arguing, I would just show him.

I learned to breathe on my own, and how to swallow, which was necessary for the feeding tube to come out. Eating solid foods started with Jell-O, mashed potatoes, and pudding. I practiced walking up and down the halls with a walker.

This is a miracle.

I spent five more days in the rehab unit, which was remarkably shorter than the weeks they had predicted.

This is a miracle.

That word was starting to irritate me. It might have seemed like a miracle to them, but to me it just felt like grindingly hard work. And the progress was coming much more slowly than I wanted. If this was such a miracle, why wasn't my healing happening in hours instead of days?

In physical therapy, I relearned how to climb stairs and lift light objects. There also were lessons in personal self-care—showering and using the bathroom by myself.

Looking in the mirror, I saw myself for the first time in many weeks. I had been admitted as a bald cancer patient, without even eyebrows. Now, I had hair. Lots of hair. The steroids that had helped keep me alive while I was on life support had turned me into Sasquatch—blond hair growing out of my ears and nose, hair all over my face . . . hair everywhere. Coming into the hospital, I was smooth top to bottom. Coming out of the coma, I was downright furry.

The good news? The mani-pedi Sarah had given me weeks earlier was perfectly intact. The nurses complimented my lovely nails just about every day.

That was great, but I was a lot more concerned about getting a razor!

When you lose a month of your life, the drive to get back to normal can be overpowering. I'm a fighter, and my first instinct was to fight to get back to the life I'd lost for an entire month. I did not want to miss a single moment of my life.

The final test I had to pass in rehab before I could go home was making a meal for myself. I chose to make a peanut butter and jelly sandwich. I reached my arms up high to the cabinet to grab the jars of peanut butter and jelly. Each item felt like it weighed one hundred pounds. My body was weak all over; my legs and arms were like jelly. My hands trembled as I slowly made the sandwich, determined to prove I was ready and able to go home.

It was the hardest darn meal I ever made in my life. Ever!

After that ordeal, I slept for several hours just to recover my strength.

And my butt was sore. I had been telling the nurses and my doctor that something was hurting back there, but no one saw anything. Even X-rays did not reveal a problem.

Somehow, even though I was running a low-grade fever, I managed to get discharged from rehab twenty-five days after coming out of the coma.

It was a cold, dreary November day. When I stepped outside, the cold took my breath away. My muscles were so weak I was barely able to get into the car. Shivering from cold and weakness, I remembered that I'd had on flip-flops that awful day when I'd been admitted six weeks earlier. A season had passed. I'd missed my birthday. A part of my life had been taken from me.

My butt hurt so badly on the ride home. I was trembling and deep down I knew it was more than just weakness. Something was wrong. My intuition told me that I was starting to go back downhill. But I remembered the last time I'd felt this way—right before I went into the hospital, at the beginning of this nightmare. There was no way in the world I was telling anyone that I felt as bad as I did. I was going home. This nightmare was over.

Todd drove fast because he knew I was really impatient to get home, but he tried to miss the bumps in the road. I was in intense pain and was miserable. Little did I know that I had an infection from a bedsore.

When I walked through the front door, I saw a huge "Welcome Home, Mommy!" sign, with cards and balloons that filled the room. Megan ran into my arms, and we hugged gently as she proudly showed me the sign she'd made.

"I love it, sweet girl," I whispered. "Thank you so much."

Gradually, the surreal nightmare of being in a coma and on life support was becoming more real. For weeks, family and friends had been fervently praying for this time to come—for me to walk into my home and embrace my sweet little girl again. But because I had this gnawing in my gut that something wasn't right, that another shoe would be dropping soon, I could barely enjoy this moment of triumph. And there was no way I was going to verbalize my fears. After all, they hadn't fully diagnosed what had put me in the hospital in the first place. Whatever it had been, I thought, I was not going back there. I felt sick, but I refused to acknowledge it to myself, much less anyone else.

This was not happening. Not again.

I turned to my husband. "I need to lie down. I don't feel well."

He helped me into bed, and I lay there in pain. Something was not right. My entire body hurt; my butt was hot, and my nerves were on fire. Yet, I refused to tell anyone.

I am not *going back to the hospital!*

The next morning, my fever spiked. A fever, I remembered, was what had placed me in the hospital the first time.

God, this cannot be happening! Please God, I cannot go back to the hospital.

I went to see my oncologist. He discovered that I had an abscess on my backside from lying still in the hospital bed for so many weeks.

"You need to be seen by a surgeon, now!" he said. "If this infection gets into your blood stream, it could kill you."

"I am not going back to the hospital. Please don't take me back there!" I begged.

I could tell from the expression on his face that my oncologist sympathized with my fear.

"It depends on where Dr. Weston is today," he said, referring to the surgeon who had performed the biopsy of my lymph node and later put in my chemo port.

Fortunately, Dr. Weston happened to be in his office, which was close by. When he saw the abnormally large, deep abscess, he quickly said I needed to be sedated to have it lanced and drained. And sedation would mean going to the hospital.

However, he also admitted that I didn't have much time before the infection grew dangerously deadly.

The nurse injected local anesthesia, but it wasn't enough to counteract the excruciating pain of dealing with that infected abscess. I've endured labor pains and, trust me, this was way worse! Thank goodness, Mom and my friend Sarah were there to hold me while I screamed like bloody murder on the table.

I left the doctor's office with a huge bandage on my backside and lots of pain meds to take. I laid across the backseat of the car on the way home. Sitting was terribly uncomfortable for months to come.

In fact, *I* felt uncomfortable for months to come—not just physically, but emotionally.

I continued to feel frightened. Numb at times. And I felt so vulnerable, not trusting that the worst was behind me.

With this setback, I needed more help than I might have asked for. Mom came and decorated the tree for me, hoping it would get me in the Christmas spirit. All I could do was lie on the couch and watch. Megan wanted to wait on me when my whole purpose in fighting to get home had been to take care of her. And in our little talks I began to understand just how much she had stuffed her feelings and tried to disappear into the woodwork while I was in the coma, because she didn't want anyone taking care of her when they needed to be taking care of me. She had taken on so much at such a young age, and it made me terribly sad.

On top of all that, my taste buds had been damaged by the ventilator and I had no appetite, so it wasn't easy getting my strength back.

Everyone who visited me did so with such hope and excitement on their faces. They all seemed to want to hear how I was looking at life differently now, how much more alive I felt after beating death.

"Oh, yes," I'd say, pulling out the best smile I could. "It's great!"

I was fighting depression and shame at a time when everyone in my life expected me to feel joyful and grateful.

They all wanted to hear about the miracle. All I could see was that I'd been through hell.

～ ～ ～

I spent the first month of 2010 going for daily radiation—twenty rounds total. I was starting to get my life back, but I was still in a lot of shock from my traumatic hospitalization. While I was getting my radiation treatments, I often prayed, asking God to heal me completely. I was grateful for all that God had done. But I still had fears of not having a full recovery.

Although I had not finished my chemotherapy treatments, the oncologist told me I was done. He said more chemo was too risky after what I'd been through, so he hoped the pre-scheduled radiation would put me in remission.

And, of course, it did! God performed yet another miracle. I had not been able to complete all my chemo treatments, yet I was cured.

This is a miracle!

The bitter truth is that it took me two years to fully get over everything my body had been through. Although I eventually adopted the story of the miracle that everyone seemed to be attaching to me, I had a long way to go. I had nothing left, emotionally or physically. I was depleted from the shock and the trauma of what had happened to me.

I was even going through the motions with God.

Now that I was no longer sick, my prayer life and my relationship with God had become stagnant. Most mornings I would read through a daily devotional and a few Scripture verses, but that was about it. Time with God was becoming more of a routine, something I checked off my list, instead of a lifeline I relied on. The Fully Rely on God Linda had gradually slipped away.

I even stopped seeing my counselor because I was tired of talking about the whole cancer ordeal; instead at all cost I avoided feeling anything about my illness. It was too fresh and I was still in shock from the hospitalization and coma.

But I did a great job of hiding all that from everyone around me.

৵ ৵ ৵

After the last day of radiation, I stopped at a restaurant to have lunch with a friend. We were celebrating the victory: cancer officially was behind me. No more treatments. I had survived a coma *and* cancer. There was no looking back. The fight was over, and it was time to start living again.

Glancing down at the counter at the checkout register, I saw a purple brochure for the Leukemia and Lymphoma Society Team In Training program. Curious, I picked it up and read these words: "Participate and save lives. Today is the day you'll start helping to save the lives of blood cancer patients by joining Team In Training (TNT) and raising money for blood cancer research."

The brochure was about a training program to run a half marathon to support blood cancer research. I couldn't believe it.

Without the slightest hesitation, I knew I was in. Even though my body was still recovering from chemo, the coma, and the radiation, I was going to find whatever it took to run 13.1 miles.

With the brochure in hand, I left the restaurant and wept in my car in amazement. Never could I have imagined that the very day I crossed the finish line in the fight for my life I would commit to crossing a very different kind of finish line.

CHAPTER TEN

LACING UP MY RUNNING SHOES for the first Team In Training meeting in May, I reflected on the perfectness of the timing: May marked the one-year anniversary of my cancer diagnosis. Also, it had been six months since my hospitalization. And, I would have six months to train to run 13.1 miles in the Virginia Beach Rock 'n' Roll Half Marathon.

The half marathon itself would take place exactly one year after I was put into a coma.

Imagine that. One year after the doctors said I had barely a 5 percent chance of survival, I planned to run a half marathon.

One year after waking up from that coma to the news that I might never walk or breathe on my own again, I would run 13.1 miles.

Oh, yes. I was definitely going to do this thing.

What hadn't occurred to me, as the first months of the new year flew by, was how much rigorous physical training it would take to run 13.1 miles.

My mom was not too happy that I was taking on such a lofty challenge so soon after nearly dying.

"Linda, I don't think it's a wise idea to put your body through such intense training after all that you went through," she said, pausing to look for signs that she could change my mind. "I don't know if your immune system can handle it so soon."

I knew she was being protective of me, as any mother would.

Todd, Megan, my friends, and doctors were supportive and inspired by my ambition.

Running a half marathon had been on my bucket list for years, even though I wasn't a real runner. I had run a little here and there over the years, but never trained for any type of event. In fact, I never sat down and made an official bucket list, but I had a checklist of experiences in my mind—mostly from conversations with Todd and my girlfriends—about things I wanted to do someday. Things that were totally out of my comfort zone. Things that amazing people with amazing lives did. That's what a half marathon had always represented to me.

Driving up to meet the training team on the first day, I was enthusiastic to take on the challenge. I hadn't done any strenuous exercise since my illness, but the coaches were going to train me, and I was ready. Despite everything that had happened to me— maybe because of everything that had happened to me—I was an overcomer. I was ready to take on the world.

However, despite everything that had happened to me, I still hadn't learned that I had nothing to prove in order for people to love me, or in order to be worthy of God's love.

The best part about training with Team In Training was their incredible support. The coaches set up water and Gatorade stops every couple of miles along the course at every practice. They even taught us how to fuel our bodies while running with GU, a "delicious" energy gel. We started and completed each training run as a team. The serious runners, who were really fast and way out in front, would come back through the course and support the slower runners with high fives and "Go team!" cheers.

When I arrived the first day, about twenty men and women were decked out in running gear. Three coaches welcomed the team. Everyone was friendly. Right away we felt like a family. We were together for a common goal. We gathered in a circle as the coaches shared inspiring stories about why we run as a team.

"Every step, every mile, represents a life you are saving," Coach Beth said.

I didn't know that every four minutes someone is diagnosed with a blood cancer. Or that every ten minutes someone dies from it. It was hard to wrap my mind around such alarming statistics, even though I am one of them. But with organizations such as the Leukemia and Lymphoma Society funding research for blood cancers and providing cancer patients and their families with support, I believe without a shadow of a doubt there will be a cure one day.

I was moved to tears as I thought about all the people who had run for the Leukemia and Lymphoma Society and how God used them as part of my miracle.

Countless miles saved my life, too.

The coaches asked each of us to share why we joined the team. When they got to me, I was in a pool of tears. Briefly I shared about the last year of my life. I also told them that I was running in memory of my mother-in-law, who passed away from multiple myeloma, a type of blood cancer.

The teammates hugged me, and I became another reason why they were running.

"It's time to get to business," Coach Jim spoke up. "Today you will run the shortest distance of the season: two miles."

Two miles. I panicked. My "just do it" mentality deflated instantly. *You've got to be kidding me! I will die.*

To me, two miles might just as well have been twenty.

I had never considered myself a runner. I'd never got up early in the morning, like some people, to run.

I had been a wannabe runner in my mind for many years—those women always looked so strong, so in control. So slender. But, I had also thought those little stick figures must be crazy, running on the side of the road in the heat of the day.

I'm not sure if I can run five minutes, much less two miles, I thought. *Oh my, I think I've gotten myself in a little too deep here. I just got through cancer. I almost died. What am I trying to prove?*

Reasoning had always been my worst enemy. Negative voices began to crowd my mind.

Go ahead. Quit now. Everyone will understand. Nobody wants you to push yourself too much and have a relapse.

Before I ever took my first step, I had run through every logical excuse to quit right then and there. However, quitting wasn't quite that simple. Two girlfriends, Stephanie and Dina, had signed up, too, to support me. One of the things I'd always loved about these two was that they did not run their lives on emotions, like I have a tendency to do.

Stephanie and Dina were two of the most rock-solid women I knew. They exuded strength. They consistently poured tons of confidence into me, especially on days when I was feeling inadequate. And when I was ready to throw in the towel, they motivated me to keep moving forward no matter how much I wanted to quit. And that wasn't just for running; that was in all areas of my life, whether in my career, relationships, or physically. You name it and Stephanie and Dina were there for me.

Our first training was in the suburbs of south Charlotte. The Ballantyne area is covered with sidewalks and lots of hills. Jogging up that first hill, my legs felt like lead. Thank goodness for Stephanie and Dina's encouragement.

"Look at you go, girl. Cancer has nothing on you. You are rocking it!"

Their comments eased the blow of my intimidated ego. Everyone else was much faster than I was and did not appear tired or worn out like me. I was the last one to finish, taking at least half an hour.

My body, still recovering from all the drugs and toxins (not to mention the paralytic drug), somehow got me to the end of that first two miles.

Training consisted of meeting with the team and coaches on Tuesday evenings and Saturday mornings. We trained at various locations, including a YMCA track, surrounding hilly neighborhoods and local parks. Stephanie and Dina faithfully showed up at every practice.

For the other days of the week, we followed a workout schedule the coaches gave us. Mondays, Wednesdays, and Thursdays consisted of the cross-training of our choice: activities such as biking, swimming, yoga, etc. We took Fridays off to allow our bodies to rest before our long runs on Saturday mornings. Each week they added miles to our Saturday runs until we made it to 13.1 for race day.

One of the Tuesday nights, about a month into training, the weather was horrible. June was hot and humid; it felt like I was in a sauna, and my lungs were not happy about it. That night the team met to run hills and do core strength exercises. It was brutal. We ran for half an hour, up and down what I believe to be the steepest hill I've ever seen in my life. Then we hit the field for drills, planks, squats, sit-ups, and God knows what else.

I was exhausted and ready to go home.

"I don't know if I can take another minute of this!" I grumbled under my breath.

But Stephanie and Dina were there. I knew I couldn't quit. They were so dedicated to be there with me. After running the hills and doing the vigorous drills, I was barely able to move, but I knew that completing the final two miles around the track was my ticket home.

As I came around the track for the last time, I started complaining, "I'm sorry, Coach, but I've gotta stop. I cannot do this last lap. I'm too tired."

"Come on, Linda. I'll run it with you," Coach Steve said. "I'll be right beside you, and we'll finish it together."

I was rolling my eyes and panting like a dog, but I agreed to finish.

"Linda, remember when you had cancer?"

"Yeah."

"What did you want more than anything when you were laid up in bed?"

I didn't answer him but instead sped up my pace.

"That's what I thought," he said. "You can do this, Linda! You've got it."

He reminded me of how strong I really was, and his words encouraged me to keep going. I was sick of listening to the chatter in my head telling me to quit. As I persevered and ran that last lap with my coach, tears welled up in my eyes.

Drenched with sweat, I accepted a hug from my coach.

"Great job, Linda! I knew you had it in you."

There is no way I ever would have finished that lap if it were not for him. Coach Steve not only moved me past my physical obstacles, he talked me through my mental hurdles.

Sometimes we need that special someone, like a coach, to come alongside us and champion our mind-set. It's been proved time and time again that we are what we think. If we think we can't, generally we can't.

And don't.

I love what Joyce Meyer says: "Miracles come in cans, not can'ts."

A little over halfway through the training, sometime in July, I ran the longest I'd ever run in my life: eight miles. Because this was the longest run so far, I was struggling. When I was almost at the end of the run, literally having less than a quarter mile left, I didn't think I could make it. I could see the team just around the corner because I was always the last to finish, but it did not matter. I was done. I thought I was going to die. There was no way I could rally any more strength to go the last few yards.

After making it through cancer and a coma, I thought, this is how I'm going to die? Will my tombstone read, "God bless her soul. She ran to the very end."

I started yelling at my teammates, "I can't do this, guys. I can't take another step." I was fed up and angry with myself. "I've gotta stop here—I quit. This is much harder than cancer!"

"Come on, Linda. It's just right there. You can do this," my teammates encouraged me.

"I'm going to tell everybody I know, if you think cancer is hard, try Team In Training," I yelled back at them, gasping the words out.

Through my tears, with my legs barely moving, I started laughing uncontrollably. My teammates burst out laughing with me.

A few minutes later, I fell to the ground at the finish line, laughing through my tears to all the cheers of my teammates. I was filled with the joy of doing something I did not believe I could do.

To this day, the team has an inside joke about me. Their inspirational signs that are put out on the training course to motivate new participants have my picture. The signs read, "If Linda can beat cancer, you can keep running!"

❧ ❧ ❧

One Saturday in August, I was unable to meet the team for my long run, so I decided to run on my own. Because I thought I would need a little moral support to get through all my miles, I asked Catherine to drive by and check on me. As I was just about to my halfway point, I heard Catherine beeping her horn behind me.

"You can do it! You go, girl! Woo-hoo!" yelled Catherine out her window. There's nothing in the world like an attaboy for motivation in the middle of a long run at 6 o'clock in the morning.

After she drove by, I felt like a million bucks. Confidently, I stepped up my pace just a bit faster. Heart racing, sweat dripping, grinning from ear to ear, I felt like an Olympian just about to cross the finish line.

Then, splat! I fell flat on my face.

An uneven spot on the sidewalk had tripped me up. With knees skinned and palms bloody, I lay on the ground searching for my cell phone. Thank goodness, Catherine was not too far away. I called her in tears, and she quickly turned around and came to my rescue.

Sobbing, I crawled into her car.

"Why me? Why does everything happen to me? I'm just trying to do something good for myself," I moaned pathetically. I pulled the visor down to check out my face in the mirror. "I have a black eye! I cannot believe this. How does someone get a black eye while running?"

I bawled my eyes out to Catherine, while she patted my arm in reassurance.

I was embarrassed. Humiliated. Mortified.

I didn't know which I felt more. I really, really, really wanted to quit that day. I kept thinking that I had given every ounce of myself, physically and mentally, to this training, and I was over it. I was tired of trying to prove myself. But I had come way too far to quit.

After getting home and cleaning up, I sat and thought some more. I didn't choose cancer, but I had chosen to sign up for this. Team In Training was helping me regain control. It was helping me reclaim responsibility for what was going on with my body. Running was *my* choice! I was determined to finish strong.

At the time I did not understand what I was trying to prove except that I could physically run a half marathon and that cancer had no more control over my body. Only later would I come to realize this race was also another tactic to convince myself that I was worthy to be alive.

∾ ∾ ∾

About twenty of my teammates and I left for Virginia Beach on Friday of Labor Day weekend in 2010.

The race was to be on September 5—another important five for me. Since painting the abstract heart that day during chemo, with that cryptic number five almost hidden inside the heart, the number had been important in my life. The number five is mentioned in Scripture more than three hundred times. It symbolizes God's grace, goodness, and favor. Oddly, in my original outline for this book, the story of painting the heart was to be in Chapter Four. But as the book evolved, that story ended up being in Chapter Five. The deadline for this manuscript was January 5, 2015.

So the date of the race felt like a good omen for me, a subtle sign from God that all would be well.

∾ ∾ ∾

During the Saturday night banquet before the event, we were recognized for our fundraising and physical training achievements. I personally had raised over two thousand dollars. Some teammates were running in memory of a loved one they had lost to cancer; others were there honoring a family member or friend that had survived cancer. Guest speakers, most of them cancer survivors and past Team In Training participants, acknowledged their heartfelt thanks for our commitment to the Leukemia and Lymphoma Society. It was a humbling, yet honoring, experience to sit in a room with hundreds of people from around the country who had joined together in the fight against blood cancer. An unspoken unity of genuine compassion among us filled the air.

Our team coaches reminded us to set our alarms quite early for the next morning: 4:00 A.M. We needed to meet in the hotel lobby at 5:00 A.M. to leave for the race together.

I slept on and off that night. I kept tossing and turning, because I was so excited about the race. It was going to be a defining moment in my life. It felt like I was giving cancer one final punch in the face. I was officially the winner, and cancer was the loser.

Finally, I fell into a really deep sleep.

The next thing I knew, Todd was shaking me and yelling, "Linda, Linda, wake up now! You overslept."

I jumped straight up out of bed. It was pitch dark.

"What? Oh, no! This can't be happening!"

I had sat my alarm clock for 4:00 P.M. instead of 4:00 A.M.

"It's okay. Your coach called, and the team is waiting on you downstairs," Todd said.

Thank God, I had my clothes laid out. I threw them on and ran out of the hotel room.

"Megan and I will see you on the course, honey!" Todd yelled after me. "We love you! You can do this!"

I flew to the elevator, with my husband, once again, cheering me on as the support of my life.

Race day finally had arrived, even though it still felt like the middle of the night as we drove a few miles to the event location. We all staggered off the bus, trying to calm our nervous excitement. I was ticked off because I had missed my coffee due to being late. After moaning and groaning to my team about not having my morning coffee, Garrett, a teammate, left the start line to find coffee for me.

"Garrett, I cannot thank you enough!" I said, giving him a hug and taking a long swallow. "Coffee is not only a beverage; it's my liquid sanity."

Now I would be able to focus on what I was there to do.

As I put on my running shoes the morning of September 5, I hoped the 13.1 miles I was about to run were going to profoundly change my life. I wasn't exactly sure what was about to happen on that course in Virginia Beach, but I sensed in my spirit that God was up to something. I whispered a little prayer, thanking God for the ability to breathe and run.

If only the doctors could see me now, I thought. Their words echoed in my mind, "She will never breathe or walk again on her own."

Thank you, Jesus. Thank you, Jesus, for miracles.

That morning I also thought about my sweet mother-in-law, Judy, passing away after her four-year battle with cancer in 2007. She had agreed to participate in a clinical-research trial across the country to help find new treatments for future cancer patients. The doctors had not given Judy a long life expectancy. Because she knew she was going to die, she wanted to make the most out of her final years. And what better way than to help others through a research trial.

Six weeks after her initial treatment, I flew out to Arkansas to help care for her. Judy was not only my mother-in-law; she also was my very best friend. For years, I talked with her on the phone several times a day. Judy knew me inside and out.

Walking down the corridor to her room, I saw a tiny old lady hunched over and barely able to walk. She looked pitiful. My heart broke into a million pieces. At that time, I remember being unable to understand what it was like for these brave people to undergo such harsh treatments. A few more steps forward and I gasped. The stooped-over old woman was Judy. Within six short weeks, she had gone from a vibrant fifty-eight-year-old woman to a fragile little bird who looked like she had aged twenty years.

In that hallway, I had committed to myself that I would take whatever steps necessary to relieve other patients' suffering. Now I realized that this race would be my first big step in finally fulfilling my commitment.

This is for you, Judy. I love you. I know you're watching over me.

I looked around at the thousands of people waiting to start running, chattering, moving to keep warm and to deal with the pent-up energy of waiting for the race to begin. I was excited to be here on this chilly morning. I felt like I was a part of something big, something remarkable. Everyone with Team In Training was decked out in their gear and was there to make a difference.

The starting gun went off.

I started running side by side with my teammates and hundreds of Team In Training participants. Most of the thousands of runners at the Rock 'n' Roll Half Marathon were there for an endurance event, but we were on the course for so much more—to support people who were literally fighting for their lives.

The first four miles I felt like I was running on air. I felt light and strong. I checked my watch and I had an excellent pace. I had trained for this the last six months. All the days I had been ready to quit were now a vague memory. I was on an adrenaline high from all the excitement of the fans cheering on the sidelines and the bands playing.

As I headed into mile five, one of my coaches on the sidelines yelled, "Go team! You got this, Linda. You got this!"

I had been warned that mile five would be a little difficult, because there would be fewer fans. This was about the time the course would cut through Camp Pendleton, a Marine Corps base. As I headed around the corner to enter the barracks, the surroundings looked a little familiar, even though I was certain I had never been on the base before.

As I turned another corner, I saw the barracks lined up on both sides of the street and instantly knew I had definitely been on this base, on this street before.

Oh, my God, I was here. I was right here.

Stunned by what I was seeing, I stopped and dropped to my knees.

My teammates stopped, too, and kneeled beside me. They were frightened.

"Linda, what's wrong?"

"Do you need help?"

"I've been here before," I cried, trying to catch my breath. "I was here when I was in my coma. I remember being right here."

During my coma, I had seen these barracks. Had been in them, trapped, unable to escape. I realized, on my knees in front of the actual barracks at Camp Pendleton, that God had been showing me this scene, maybe as both a metaphor and as a promise. A metaphor for the way I had felt throughout my coma—trapped in a place I didn't understand. And a promise that I would fight my way out of it, a foretelling that I would be here, on this street, someday, fully recovered.

Still feeling emotionally staggered by this realization of how God had communicated to me when everyone around me thought I was beyond reach, I let my friends help me back up to my feet. I starting jogging slowly, staring in pure amazement at my surroundings.

"I was there. I was right there." I kept pointing and telling everyone running around me.

It was surreal. It was eerie . . . and, yet, comforting at the same time.

Somehow I managed to get back to my previous running pace, even though the experience was like having just seen a ghost. A supernatural knowing quieted my spirit and reassured me that I had been in the hands of God the entire time I was in the fight for my life—from the moment I found out I had a mass behind my heart to every hour I lay in the hospital bed, balanced between heaven and earth.

As I ran, I was comforted to realize God had me, even when I did not have him.

That day was not the last time I had such an encounter. I've continued to experience, or relive, other memories from my coma—a trip to Boston, a spa in California, even shopping for pottery with a friend, all places and scenes that came flooding back to me when I experienced them for the first time after recovering.

I don't have these encounters frequently, but from time to time out of nowhere I'll have a flashback. I don't believe I will ever fully understand it on this side of eternity. I don't believe this is something I need to understand or try to figure out.

As I continued along the course, I was exhilarated. This was one of the greatest accomplishments in my life by far. There was no greater feeling than pushing through pain to experience victory. Every stride I made was bringing me one step closer to the life God intended for me all along. And in recognizing that God had shown me the military base during my coma, I felt strongly that

God had been preparing me for this moment. Even when there was barely any breath in my lungs, God had been preparing me to run this half marathon.

> [What the enemy tried to use] to harm me, God intended it for good to accomplish what is now being done. (Gen. 50:20)

Sprinting toward the finish line, I could hear Todd and Megan cheering for me on the sidelines, just as they did when I was on life support. They had never stopped believing God could do the impossible. Their faith came full circle.

God was redeeming all the pain, trauma, and heartache my family had experienced over the last year with every stride I made. No more cancer. No more fear.

As I crossed the finish line, my arms flew up in the air. With sweat and tears pouring down my face, I fell into Todd's and Megan's arms.

Thank you, God! Thank you, God!

> I press on to reach the end of the race and receive the heavenly prize for which God, through Christ Jesus, is calling us. (Phil. 3:14 NLT)

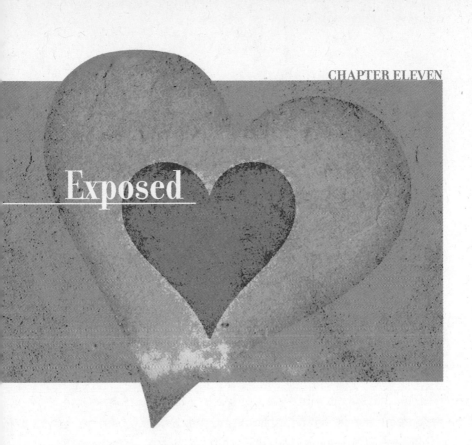

CHAPTER ELEVEN

Exposed

HIGH OFF THE VICTORY OF FINISHING the half marathon, I was on fire to tell everyone about the miracle God had performed in my life.

I felt in control. I had been able to push air through my lungs for nearly three hours, and I had experienced the strength of my legs carrying me forward for more than thirteen miles. *This*—after five months of chemotherapy, four weeks of radiation, and six weeks in the hospital, three of them in a coma—was my story.

The idea of motivating others to overcome their obstacles came to me while receiving such passionate training from my running coaches. Their words of encouragement literally lifted me off the pavement many times. While training, I discovered a God-given passion deep in my soul—coaching. What my coach did for me the night when he wouldn't let me quit—and many other times during training—was what I could not wait to do for other people. I knew that was how I would spend the rest of my life, loving and encouraging women all over the world to achieve their God-given potential.

Shortly after the half marathon, I attended Christian Coach Institute to become a Certified Christian Life Coach. A year later I started my online coaching practice and began speaking to women's groups at churches, as well as coaching women in one-on-one sessions.

I had never done any type of professional speaking before; however, I felt comfortable sharing my story from the very start. My "miracle" story was the lifeblood of my message.

I was passionate with every word, every pause, and every facial expression. It was well rehearsed. I was good. I was really good. And my story was amazing; it was riveting. Audiences of women were enthralled and held on to every word.

At the time, I just thought women were hungry to hear about a miracle. When I would see them wiping tears from their eyes, I never fully understood why they had so much emotion. They didn't really know me, so why did they care that I was still alive?

As I continued to tell my story over and over, often I would wait in anticipation for their tears to come to feel affirmed, validated . . . worthy to be alive.

Dancing in a desperate need for approval, I filled my calendar with speaking engagements, blogging, coaching, and volunteering. My hustle for worthiness was disguised in the perfect Christian mask of "sharing God's love with others."

But my new label—"She's a miracle!"—began to mock me.

You aren't a miracle.

Whenever I told the story, I walked away from the conversation almost embarrassed by the attention and the way people received my story—sometimes with awe or reverence or joy.

You aren't a miracle! You aren't special!

The belittling voices I'd struggled with so much of my life were back with a vengeance.

Whenever cancer came up—in the checkout line at the grocery store, with people I didn't even know—I would find myself telling my story. It was almost as if telling the story often enough might eventually shut up those ugly voices in my head.

You're just doing this for attention.

It was as if the story of my healing was a floodlight shining directly in my face. My reaction was to squint, look away, cover my eyes. Believing I was worthy of a miracle was a light too bright for me to look at it directly.

I fell prey to the enemy's lies all over again.

Eventually, the lies grew even darker. Not only was I not worthy of a miracle, I even began to believe I did not deserve to be alive and healthy. How did I earn the right to survive cancer? A darling little eight-year-old girl in my neighborhood, Ellie, lost her battle to cancer shortly after my hospitalization. Why did I deserve to live and not her?

Eventually, whenever someone around me uttered the word "miracle," my stomach began to turn. My chest would feel like it might collapse. I felt certain I was lying to myself as I told everyone my story. I felt like a fake. A hypocrite.

But I kept sharing my story, secretly hoping every time I told it that I would believe it myself. Believe that I was worthy of a miracle.

Instead, each time I felt more and more ashamed. I was imprisoned by self-condemnation.

Shame convinced me I was unlovable. It told me, *You're a disappointment.* I felt like a failure.

For nearly two years, I lived a double life. On the outside, I appeared to be a happy wife and mother, the resilient cancer and coma survivor with a successful Christian coaching business. On the inside, I was drifting farther away from God. My faith was fading. I began to question if I really believed in God, to question if the God I now doubted had anything to do with my healing. Maybe I just got lucky. Maybe I just had the right medical team.

I continued to read daily devotionals or Christian blogs. I went to church regularly. I even prayed with my clients. But my heart was disconnected. I was all about the doing and not just simply being.

And because I wasn't *being*, the *doing* felt fake.

～～～

I started to live every day in fear of being exposed—having the world discover that I was never worthy of a miracle.

The day it happened I was speaking at a typical event, a women's Bible study group, in the home of a pastor's wife, with about a dozen women excited to hear my story. A Muslim woman who lived next door showed up as well, wanting to hear about my miracle firsthand. I was treated like royalty: A welcome sign honored me. The dining room table was set with beautiful flowers. The food was delicious. I knew how it would go: We would have a time of prayer and worship, even some laughter. Everyone would leave on cloud nine.

That's how it always went. But that isn't how it went that day.

Everyone was eager to hear about my miraculous healing. As I shared every detail of God's goodness, the women hung on every word. Their faces showed signs of belief and hope. At the end of my talk I opened it up for Q&A.

"I bet you see life differently now after all you have been through. What is that like for you?"

I could slide through that question so easily now. "You know, it's great!" I would gush. "I'm just grateful to be alive. I'm grateful to be here for my daughter."

I smiled. They smiled. They believed it, of course, because isn't that how everyone would feel?

"How are your husband and daughter after all of this?"

"They've been through a lot," I would say, as I always did. "Even to this day they don't talk a lot about it."

A few women would nod, as if they could imagine what it would be like for their husband and children, too.

"Tell us, what was it like being in a coma?" Sometimes the women who asked this question were asking out of curiosity; other times, you could see in their eyes that they asked because they were troubled or fearful or hopeful. This woman was one of the latter. "Could you hear people talking to you?"

"Actually, I heard my mother's voice only once, and she was by my bedside every single day," I said, smiling and hoping to reassure her. "The interesting thing is when and how I heard her."

I told them about the day my friend Sarah stopped by to visit after I returned home from the hospital. I was glad to see her because I'd wanted to ask her about her fiancé Jason's visit while I was in a coma. He was the one person I could clearly remember talking to me while I was comatose.

"You must be thinking of somebody else," Sarah told me. "Jason never visited you when you were in the coma."

I'd been pouring us a cup of coffee and my hands froze. "Are you sure?"

"I promise. I'd remember if he had."

I told my audience that I'd been positive Sarah was wrong because I remembered Jason's visit so clearly, so vividly. It was one night when I was panicked, terrified that I was about to die. I remembered that I was physically fighting to stay alive.

"Then, out of nowhere, I heard Jason's voice." The audience grew very still when I reached this point in the story. "He told me exactly what to do so I wouldn't die. His words fell over me with peace that I believe saved my life. Then he told me I shouldn't worry, that my mom had been there at the hospital with me the whole time.

"That's when I heard my mother speak my name, right after Jason told me she was there. And that was the only time I remember hearing anyone's voice."

Then I told them the rest of the story. Because Sarah was so adamant that Jason had never visited me and I was so sure he had, Sarah called him later that day. She asked her fiancé if he ever went to the hospital to see me without telling her. He said no. She pressed him to be sure. When he asked why, she told him.

When Jason heard the story, he began to cry.

"The night the doctors gave her less than a 5 percent chance of survival," he said between his tears, "I prayed that God would let me talk to her. God gave me words of peace to speak to her."

He had never been in the room with me, but God had answered his prayers by allowing him to speak words of healing straight to me despite my coma.

The women were in awe: God had performed yet another miracle!

After the event wrapped up and I was receiving hugs and saying my goodbyes, one of the women who approached me was a poised and polished woman in her forties who just so happened to be a doctor. She had a somewhat concerned look on her face. Looking tenderly into my eyes, she said, "Linda, as you were sharing your testimony, something in my spirit stopped me. When you were talking about your hospitalization, your expression—or more like your belief—shifted. It was as though you were trying to convince yourself that God really did heal you. Linda, you don't *believe* you were miraculously healed."

Although there was nothing in her voice or her expression that was accusatory, my heart sank, and every nerve in my body went on alert. I felt like I'd been caught with my hand in the cookie jar—exposed as the "nice church lady gone bad." I wanted to look away from her, as she waited for my response.

I cleared my throat and swallowed hard. "Thank you for sharing this with me," I managed to say. "I definitely will spend some time in prayer about this."

Turning quickly, I left and headed to my car. I could not hide fast enough. Over and over again, her words played in my mind.

You don't believe you were miraculously healed.

On one hand, I was ticked off by her accusation.

You don't believe you were miraculously healed.

On the other hand, I knew she was absolutely right.

While I sat in the car trying to process what I was feeling, a hot rush of emotions flooded my body. My face reddened. My hands started sweating. I could barely catch my breath.

That woman is crazy! Who is she to tell me that? It's a bunch of crap. She doesn't know me, and she doesn't know what I've been through. Who is she to question what I believe?

The truth is, my head was swirling and my body was reacting so violently because I'd just heard someone say out loud what I had been quietly telling myself for months.

Finally, realizing the other cars had already left, I put down the convertible top on my VW bug, quickly pulled out of the parking lot and headed for home. I tried shaking off my tumultuous emotions but found myself on a too-familiar spiritual roller coaster. Having ridden high to the top of the mountain, I was now speeding straight down to the deep, dark valley.

Instead of praying, I resorted to speed dial and called a friend.

"It was amazing!" I gushed, stuffing my shame and anger from my accuser's words. "God was there today. I wish you could have seen their faces. They were in awe of God's miracle. Days like today are why I'm still alive—I just know it!"

"Oh, my sweet friend, you truly are a miracle," my friend responded.

That word again!

When I got home and pulled into my driveway, I sat dazed, unable to get out of my car and go into the house. I was paralyzed by shame.

Shame was suffocating me. I felt like I couldn't breathe again.

Shame made me want to run away, to isolate myself and wallow in my own misery.

Shame had me living in hell on earth.

Am I ever going to make it out of this nightmare?

∿ ∿ ∿

As I stumbled through the next few days, the voice in my head started asking me if I even believed in God. After all, if I believed in God, how could I not see the miracles everyone else seemed to see so clearly?

My head told me I did—I prayed, read the Bible, attended church, and led Bible studies. I drove around with my Jesus bumper sticker and filled my bookcases with books about God. I wore my Christianity like a badge of honor.

But now that I had acknowledged this doubt, it lingered.

Now that someone else had seen through me, I couldn't shake the idea that it wasn't just the miracle I doubted. It was God himself.

I was scared to death to admit to myself (much less to anyone else) that I struggled with unbelief. The thought terrified me: *What if I really am the good church lady gone bad?*

A few days later, I was on the phone with Catherine, complaining and sulking in self-pity.

"I am sick and tired of struggling," I said. "Why does my life have to be so hard?"

"Linda, God did not keep you here to struggle. He has a plan for your life," Catherine reminded me once again.

Her words were the last straw. I snapped. I came unglued.

"Catherine, I don't believe that anymore!" I screamed. "I don't believe I'm a miracle! I don't believe there's a plan for my life. I never believed it. I don't even know if I believe God is real."

I cried uncontrollably, trying to catch my breath.

With less than a five-second pause, she said, "Okay. Linda, you do not have to believe. It's okay if you don't believe."

Suddenly, the world seemed to stop spinning.

"Really? I don't have to believe, really?" The words brought release. Decades of angst eased from my body. I could breathe again.

"Yes, Linda. Nobody ever said you have to believe God is real," Catherine said.

For the first time, I felt okay with *not being okay*. With not having all the answers and not feeling certain or confident. Somewhere inside, my body rested . . . knowing everything was going to be okay.

∿ ∿ ∿

You might think that I found God immediately afterward, but that's not how it played out. Not even close.

The following six months, I ran in the opposite direction from God. I felt angry and rebellious and somewhat betrayed by the God I had just heard I didn't have to believe in. The arguments in my head bounced back and forth so rapidly that I felt dizzy with disbelief. Often I just shut down.

I put my Christian coaching business on hold, secretly hoping to never do it again. I stopped going to church. I dropped out of all ministry volunteer roles. I certainly had no desire to pray. I didn't tell anyone what was going on with me.

Determined to do life my way, I set out to get a job, anything that would provide some quick income while I figured out what I wanted to do with my life.

My first job lasted a total of four hours. Yep, four hours! I put on an apron in an upscale restaurant, only to be chewed out by customers who wore crosses around their necks and prayed before their meal. I politely resigned at the end of my first shift.

Then I worked the phones as a receptionist at a kiddie hair salon. These little ones were entertained while sitting in tiny planes, trains, and automobiles so a stylist could cut their hair. After six weeks of putting up with kicking and screaming toddlers and short-tempered stylists, I ushered myself out the door.

So for the next few months, I avoided work altogether. I bathed in self-pity and searched for happiness in self-help groups, books, and online courses. Nothing worked. I felt lonely, broken, and restless. I was operating totally on self-will and avoiding having anything to do with God.

Then, out of nowhere, another job opportunity presented itself. The pay was great, it was close to home, and it was in a field I had worked in prior to my cancer diagnosis. I believed it would provide everything I needed: a routine, a steady income, and an opportunity to live the normal American dream. I'd get up, go to work, come home, watch TV, go to bed, and do it all over again five days a week.

The next Monday morning at 8:00 I was answering phones in a pediatric dentist's office; certain that things were going to be different. I felt like I had purpose, direction, and meaning in my life once again.

On Wednesday morning at 8:00, a thought popped into my head.

Linda, you are not supposed to be here.

I dismissed it instantly, believing I had to be there. It was just another one of those crazy voices in my head. The job was the answer to all my problems. It had to work out.

A couple of days later, the office manager called me into her office. "Linda, I'm so sorry, but I made a mistake hiring you. It's not working out," she said.

With a sigh of relief, I kindly thanked her for the opportunity and readily left yet another place of employment.

I had finally reached the end of my rope. I was hesitant to call any of my friends, because I was sure they were exhausted from all my emotional ups and downs; only one person remained that I knew would listen. Driving home that day, I had a heart-to-heart, come-to-Jesus meeting with God.

God, I cannot do this anymore.

I pulled my car into a parking lot at a shopping center.

I'm exhausted.

Resting my forehead on the steering wheel, I sobbed.

If you are real, then I need you to show me you are real. I need you to come alive in my life. I want a real, intimate relationship with you.

In the car next to me, I saw two women who were laughing together as they got out of their car. I thought of Catherine and Todd and the other people who were always there for me, people who listened and comforted me and made me laugh and dried my tears. That, I thought, was what I wanted from God, what I needed from God.

I want you to be as real to me as my best friend.

If that could happen, I thought, maybe that would be the real miracle.

CHAPTER TWELVE

Encounter

INDECISION HAD TORMENTED ME long enough.

Sitting in my car in that parking lot, I decided once and for all that I was no longer going to be on the fence about this God thing. I was going to be all in and search for him with my whole heart.

I began a daily practice of prayer. My words were not bold, but they were sincere.

God, help me. Why isn't this getting through to me? Why does everybody but me see miracles in my life? Show me how to believe. Please!

I knew that, after all that I'd been given, it was irrational of me to expect God to work more miracles just so I could doubt them. *I* was the one who needed to change in order to really, truly have a relationship with God. That's when I began to get a glimmer that I needed more than saying I believed. I needed a real relationship with a living Jesus.

I began reading the Bible, but this time with curiosity. I wanted to meet the real Jesus.

> But if from there you seek the LORD your God, you will find him if you look for him with all your heart and with all your soul. (Deut. 4:29)

One morning after my family left for work and school, I sat down for quiet time with God. I didn't have any long, profound prayers left in me. I was as spiritually bankrupt as I had ever been. But I knew I had to just take some action.

"Okay, God," I said softly, so afraid nothing I could do would connect me with this God I had started to doubt. "I'm here. I'm seeking you."

That's really all I could manage that first day. But I was desperate, and I was determined. I was going to find Jesus.

I began to use devotional books that had always been my favorites. I looked up the Scripture verses. I wanted to know Jesus intimately and was ready for him to reveal himself to me. That meant I had to do my part. I had to stop waiting for the pastor to deliver an "aha!" moment. I had to stop waiting for faith on a silver platter. I had to do something!

Then I had to be willing to let God deliver the outcome.

I couldn't step up my reading and my praying in order to manipulate God into revealing himself to me. I had to simply do my part so God's grace could work in me.

I had to be honest.

I had to talk.

I had to listen.

Opening my Bible to the New Testament, I started reading in Matthew. But this time, I read it out loud. It was a little strange at first, but then I actually started enjoying it. The words coming out of my mouth were passionate—they held belief and conviction. Yes, those beliefs and convictions belonged to the earliest saints of the Christian church, not to me. But in speaking aloud their beliefs and their convictions, I found myself responding to them in a way I never had. They were no longer just flat words printed on thin sheets of paper. They were the bold declarations of living, breathing people who had walked in the company of the living, breathing Christ.

In talking their talk, I began to hear in a way I had never before heard.

And my prayers changed, too, from a formal approach to a simple conversation. I talked with God out loud throughout the day, just as if I were talking to my best friend over the phone. You know the kind of conversation I mean—those long talks with friends who know all your secrets and love you anyway, friends you can tell everything because you aren't judged, friends who want only the best for you. The kind of friends you could talk to all day long without getting bored.

The more I had those conversations, the more I was filled by this relationship with my new friend. And the more I was filled, the hungrier I grew to know him more.

Little by little, God continued showing up, and I began to see those signs of his presence. I was shocked to see things happening all around me. The prayers I planted in my heart began sprouting up everywhere. I knew they were God—only God.

One afternoon I prayed for Megan to have a desire for God's Word, and the next morning she asked me if we could start reading a devotional together and praying together before school.

Later that same week I prayed for my family to commit to regularly attending church. After we went to worship that weekend, my husband stood in the kitchen and was adamant that we needed to continue going to church regularly. It was good for the family, he said.

I giggled. *Only God.*

I began to experience joy. Not just happiness, but real joy. Happiness, I realized, was the emotion I felt when everything was working out in my life, when things went my way. But now I had joy! Even when things didn't go my way, I still had peace, hope, perspective. Joy could not be contained. And it was so much more than an emotion. It was an overflowing of the Holy Spirit coming out of my life.

Only God could deliver joy. My newfound love for Jesus and his truths began to fill me more and more . . . and to strengthen my faith. Instead of just knowing Jesus and who he *was*, I fell in love with who he *is* in my everyday life.

The simplest moments became treasured blessings. Holding my husband's hand, walking my dogs in the park, or listening to Meg talk about her favorite rock star were times when I'd find myself thanking Jesus for the gift of life. Jesus was slowing me down and showing me what was truly important in life, the simple times.

Stepping into a new phase of spiritual maturity, I found the courage to go back into Christian coaching.

> I sought the LORD, and he answered me;
>   he delivered me from all my fears. (Ps. 34:4)

~ ~ ~

One afternoon as I finished up a coaching session, something inside me felt unsettled. I couldn't quite put my finger on it, but I felt uneasy. I decided to work on an upcoming blog post to find some focus. I sat down at the kitchen table, opened my laptop, and began to write. After the first sentence, I snapped it shut.

I reached for my Bible and starting reading it out loud. Doing this felt comforting and energizing, so I stood up to pace the floor and soon felt an urge to start praying. Dressed in my everyday leggings and baggy T-shirt, I began walking around the house and praying. In every room, words flew out of my mouth. In the seven years I had lived in my house, I probably had prayed over it only once or maybe twice.

After at least twenty minutes of praying, I walked back into the kitchen and noticed a text message from the client I had spoken with earlier.

It said, *Friend, do you speak in tongues?*

I responded immediately, *No, but I believe I will one day.*

It was random. It was nothing I had ever thought about. I'm not sure why I responded that way.

She replied, *You will today.*

Quickly I typed back, *It's strange you sent me this message. I just finished praying like crazy all over my house! Something I never do.*

I found out she had been praying and singing a hymn in tongues at the very same time I had been praying around my house. She told me that she had an impression in her spirit that her words, her song were for me.

She asked me if I would like to Skype and pray together. All the way from Alaska to North Carolina we connected. God was up to something. As we prayed, we both asked for the Holy Spirit to gift me with the ability to speak in tongues, even though I had never thought much about it. The only thing I really knew about speaking in tongues was that it was mentioned somewhere in Acts around the time of Pentecost. I had heard a few people pray in tongues before, but I thought it was kind of mysterious at the time and didn't give it a second thought.

As we prayed, I got on my knees and cried. I repented for doubting God's existence after my illness.

Lord, please forgive my unbelief.

We continued to pray and talk for a few minutes. I told her that I wasn't really feeling like I was going to start speaking in tongues and that it just might not happen for me. She said that it was okay, but *when* it happened, not to be afraid or think I'm crazy.

"Just keep speaking," she said.

After ending our conversation, I closed my laptop again and sat at the table feeling a little uncertain. I wasn't a hundred percent sure what I believed about the whole speaking in tongues thing. But I opened the Bible to Psalms and read aloud, "Delight yourself in the LORD, and He will give you the desires of your heart" (Ps. 37:4 NASB).

I stood to my feet again to pray, but this time I instantly began to babble in some kind of new language. My own ears didn't understand what I was saying.

I walked through the house again, laying my hands on different objects while I prayed in this unfamiliar language.

Oh my gosh! Am I speaking in tongues? What is this?

When I went into certain rooms where I once felt a lingering heaviness from my illness, my language sped up and changed completely. I raised my hands over the painting I created when I was undergoing chemotherapy—the heart with the abstract number five—and my words changed again. As I walked over to a small delicate urn that contained my mother-in-law's ashes, a joyful laughter bubbled up as the language changed again.

I kept thinking that I might be a little whack-a-doodle. But it felt so natural.

I could not stop. I didn't want to stop.

I no longer wondered if the Holy Spirit really lived inside me. I was experiencing the "fullness of God" (Eph. 3:19). I *felt* him permeating every fiber of my being. From my central core between my heart and my lower abdomen, I experienced something tugging from within.

Never in my life had I experienced such completeness in my spirit. It felt supernatural—the ability to relate to God like never before. I was amazed at how his divine order was being reestablished in my life. I felt his Spirit ruling over my soul and body, creating wholeness. I knew that day that not only was I saved by Jesus, but I was filled with the Holy Spirit.

❧ ❧ ❧

I was in such amazement at the way I had been filled with the Holy Spirit that I could not contain myself. As soon as I picked up Megan from school, I had to tell her.

"You are never going to believe what happened to me today!"

"What?"

"I spoke in tongues! God filled me with the Holy Spirit, and I can't stop praying in this crazy language. Do you want me to pray for you?"

"Yes!"

Laying my right hand on her as I steered the wheel with my left, I began to pray. Unknown words flew out of my mouth.

"Do you know what you are saying, Mom?"

"I don't understand the words, but I have a sense that I am praying peace over you."

Laughing as we rode down the highway, I felt fully alive like never before.

I dropped Meg off at her art class and sat in my car. All I wanted to do was pray in the Spirit. I was afraid people would think I was crazy, sitting in my car all alone talking to myself, so I cupped my hand over my mouth and continued to pray nonstop. Because all of this was so new to me and I did not know a thing about it, I wondered if it would last.

Will I still have this tomorrow, or is this a temporary thing?

I took out my iPhone and recorded myself praying, just in case it disappeared. That evening when we got home from Meg's art class, I told my husband all about it and even played him the recording on my phone. Having attended a small private Methodist college, he was familiar with the spiritual gift of speaking in tongues and was just as excited as I was.

Shocked that I had received this gift, I felt almost as if I had won the spiritual lottery. As usual, I questioned why I had been given such a gift. In awe and wonder during the next couple of days, I continued to pray and dig deep into Scripture to see what the Bible had to say about tongues. I contacted a spiritual mentor and talked with her about it for hours. I began to see this gift as one of the many mysteries of faith and the Holy Spirit being manifested in my life.

To this day, the gift of praying in tongues continues to be available to me. It's a source of great joy for me and has made my experience with prayer so much more powerful. It isn't for me to understand or figure out how or why this gift was given to me and not to someone else—just as it isn't for me to understand why I was given the gift of physical healing when others aren't.

When Jesus appeared after the crucifixion he commanded his apostles,

> Do not leave Jerusalem, but wait for the gift my Father
> promised, which you have heard me speak about. For
> John baptized with water, but in a few days you will be
> baptized with the Holy Spirit. (Acts 1:4–5)

> All of them were filled with the Holy Spirit and began
> to speak in other tongues as the Spirit enabled them.
> (Acts 2:4)

∾ ∾ ∾

In the days that followed, the presence of Jesus became real to me. This, maybe more than anything others might call a miracle, has been the miracle in my life. And it's a miracle we are all worthy of, a miracle that's available to all of us. But to get there, I had to stop coming at my relationship with Jesus from a place of logic or reason. Logic and reason alone *cannot* make up your faith.

One morning, not long after my first experience of praying in tongues, I went out for one of my early morning runs. When I run, I usually go by myself because I don't like to talk while running. It's too hard. It makes me short of breath. That morning, I made a different decision: I decided to invite Jesus along for my run.

During my run, I prayed nonstop. I prayed—and ran—without effort. I could not stop praying . . . out loud. The entire three miles I never felt short of breath.

My relationship with God had shifted. It was personal.

The cry of my heart for God to become *real* was answered. I had prayed to have an intimate relationship with him, and he gave me more than I ever imagined. The presence of the Almighty God speaking through my spirit and out of my very own mouth . . . how much closer could he get?

∿ ∿ ∿

I awoke one night out of a dead sleep. I felt in my spirit a prompting to use Jesus as an acronym describing how to live my faith. I didn't have pen and paper on my bedside table, but I grabbed my iPhone and typed out the following:

- **J**ust live today.
- **E**xpect miracles.
- **S**peak truth.
- **U**se your gifts.
- **S**tart now!

Thinking that was a pretty neat acronym, I then rolled over to go back to sleep. Instead of falling asleep, I kept tossing and turning, repeating the acronym.

Hmm. How many letters spell Jesus? I counted out on my fingers . . . five.

Five. That was interesting. Five was a meaningful number to me, as you know by now. I was given a less than 5 percent chance of surviving. The five on my heart painting I made during chemotherapy flashed in my mind. The date of my half marathon—September 5. I've often heard that the number five represents God's grace. God's generous and totally unexpected and undeserved miraculous healing in my life was nothing but his pure grace.

I saved my notes about the JESUS acronym on my iPhone for more than a year. I began journaling on this acronym in the context of my life—my childhood, my cancer, the coma, my miracle, the half marathon, my coaching career, my Christian beliefs (and my unbelief), and God's redemption of it all.

Little by little this revelation about the name Jesus and how it connected, for me, with habits that drew me closer to him became a cornerstone for my spiritual practices. And after I was given the gift of tongues, I began to actively use these practices as my new habits for staying personally connected with Jesus.

In the following chapters of this book, I will share with you how I continue to build a stronger intimate relationship with Jesus in a posture of daily, intentional dependence on God.

The ways I apply these practices to my life may not be the way you apply them to your life. God made us all unique and, because of that, our relationship with Jesus and the ways we connect with him may be different. So don't judge your ways of connecting with God by mine. Don't think for one minute that you have to do exactly what I do. Try something different. Look for the pathway God sets before you. Believe me, you will know when you're connecting.

Before we move into a quick look at these practices, I must stress the main thing I have learned from the miracles in my life —and am still learning—about being a Christian. I've learned to move beyond those old false beliefs from my childhood that told me I must do something special to be worthy of God's love. That I must be perfect in order to be lovable. What my experiences have shown me is that Christianity is not about doing or following all the rules, but simply about accepting the gift of a relationship with our loving God.

Getting all caught up in trying to do the right thing often serves only to remind me of how short I fall. The only requirement God asks of us is to put our faith in Christ.

> We are made right with God by placing our faith in Jesus Christ. And this is true for everyone who believes, no matter who we are. (Rom. 3:22 NLT)

I pray that the following chapters will become an inspirational practice to deepen your awareness of Jesus and relationship with him. I hope they will help you to fully embrace the truth that you are a child of God and, therefore, worthy of his love, his care, his protection, his grace, his mercy—every good gift, in fact.

Mom and me

Todd and me at high school graduation

Me, Megan, and Judy on
Judy's first day of chemo

Me, Megan, and Todd

Bashing ceremony before the first chemo treatment

The day I shaved my head

Painting during chemotherapy

The abstract 5 within the heart has significant meaning throughout my miraculous healing.

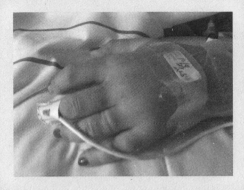

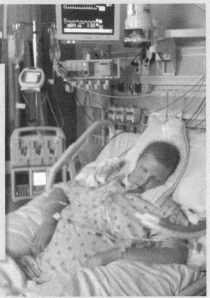

In the coma on life support

Learning to walk again

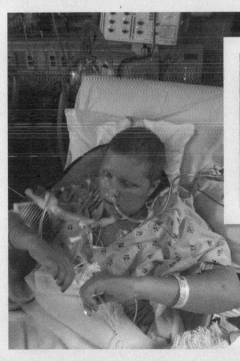

Waking up from the coma

Finished half marathon!

The bug

Part Two

CHAPTER THIRTEEN

Just Live Today

Do not worry about tomorrow, for tomorrow will worry about itself. Each day has enough trouble of its own. (Matt. 6:34)

SO MUCH TIME IS WASTED. Precious minutes, hours, days, and weeks.

Time slips by because our minds linger on what *has* happened, or we focus on what *will* happen. We worry about the past and we plan for the future. Our human nature is to try to fix old mistakes and to control what might be.

The second the alarm clock sounds, we sigh. We can't get up. Resistance tugs as we hit snooze. Then a second time . . . and a third. Wrestling with tangled sheets, we're overwhelmed with the hectic schedule of the day ahead of us before our feet ever hit the floor.

Or we jump up mindlessly, rushing headlong into our day and our to-do lists without taking a moment to acknowledge the gift of waking to a new day, breathing in and breathing out, experiencing love, laughter, and joy.

We can't wait to get through the first four hours of our workday so we can get to our lunch with friends. Or we can't wait until we get the kids off to school so we can get the laundry done, finish the grocery store run. We can't wait until we've run all those errands so we can get back to the quiet of our home. Where there's something else waiting before we can finally be content. We find ourselves repeatedly saying, "If I just get through this . . ."

Then what? Will we be satisfied?

At night, we can't wait until the dinner dishes are in the dish-washer. Can't wait until we've finished helping the kids with their homework. Can't wait until we get to bed. But when we finally lay our heads down on our pillows, our minds then scroll through all the woulda, coulda, shoulda items left over from the day.

Do you feel the tension—sometimes the downright impossi-bility—of trying to be fully present and in the moment every day? I know I do.

Often I hear people talk about how a potentially fatal illness has made them so much more aware of the importance of living each moment intentionally and fully. I've had those moments, too. But years after my own illness, I find that living right now continues to be a challenge. I want to. I mean to. I really do.

But the reality of my human nature is that it is so easy for me to slip back into fretting over the past or worrying about the future. Anything, it seems, but being in the here and now.

God instructs us not to worry about the past or the future. The Creator directs the sun and the moon, and he orders each day in his perfect plan. Every twenty-four hours is a gift—a "present" we are encouraged to accept. We have the choice to receive it and make it count.

> This is the day which the LORD has made;
> let us rejoice and be glad in it. (Ps. 118:24 NASB)

Some days I receive the gift of today. But sometimes I wake up and want to relive the day before . . . to make it better than it was. Sometimes, I wake up and my mind is already three days ahead . . . planning for that special event my family has coming up.

Oftentimes, today just seems too ordinary. Or too hectic. Or too troubled.

When I was diagnosed with cancer and was afraid I was going to die, I wanted my time back. I wanted to undo the days I'd let slip through my hands . . . the slow and sweet moments with my husband, and the simple and silly moments with my daughter. I would sit on my front porch swing with the sinking feeling (the new reality!) that I only had that very hour, that very day. I could not go backward, and I was not guaranteed a future. I just had today.

Looking back, I am finally aware of what a tremendous gift it was to recognize that all I had was that single moment.

～ ～ ～

One day recently as I was driving into my neighborhood after picking Megan up from middle school, I reached over to hold her hand. Her presence mesmerized me as she talked about her day. Listening to her giggle as she told me about the cute boy in her social studies class, I took in her every word. In that moment, I was overwhelmed in the quiet of my heart that I was able to be her mom, right then and there.

If it were not for receiving the miracle of physical and spiritual healing, I would not get to experience the holiness of my everyday life. The beauty in the simple things of life would go unnoticed. I'm still learning that life is a precious gift and I must handle it with care. I'm becoming more grateful for the simple moments.

How do you and I let go of trying to manipulate our lives and start fully embracing what's right in front of us? How do we abandon the fear of failure and past regrets? How do we temper our anticipation of the future? How do we stay connected to the present moment?

There's only one place I know to turn to, and that is to the truth: Jesus.

It starts with just living today.

But how do I *do* that?

First, let me admit that I do it imperfectly.

When I'm doing it fairly well, it starts with gratitude. I walk through my day paying attention to all that I have to be grateful for, beginning with the sunrise of a new day, these two strong legs that will take me where I need to go, the breath I can take with no assistance whatsoever, the people who love me, or perhaps a moment of unexpected laughter.

Some people become more conscious of those things by keeping a gratitude list. They may put those lists in their purse or their jeans pocket. Some people journal about such things at night. Others turn their nightly prayers into a thank-you note to God. Doing this brings gratitude to the forefront of my mind. And having gratitude in mind makes me more aware of what's right in front of me.

That is one key to just living today.

When I choose to open my eyes each morning with gratitude that the sun rose, that I can breathe, that I can walk, and talk (and, yes, I can taste—especially pizza!), then the day ahead appears less cloudy, less cluttered.

Here are my top five Just Live Today habits. Maybe some of them will become yours, too. Or maybe you'll find five of your own that work well for you.

1. Deep breathing—taking time to simply breathe.
2. Thanking, praising, and worshiping God continually throughout the day.
3. Slowing down. Not rushing through my day.
4. Being aware of how I'm feeling physically. Is there tension throughout my body?
5. Listening—to myself, to my surroundings, to God.

In the morning, LORD, you hear my voice;
 in the morning I lay my requests before you
and wait expectantly. (Ps. 5:3)

When I'm really connected with God, I'm able to be mindful of every minute, whether it's talking with Megan on the drive to school or enjoying dinner with my husband after he returns home from work. Slowing down to engage in each part of the day's routine helps me to keep my eyes focused on the now. Distractions are more easily set aside and worry disappears. I'm reminded that I don't have to know all of life's answers, because I walk by faith and not sight.

One way to live in the moment is to keep the focus on God and the fact that God is right there with you. It's impossible to dwell in

the past or the future if you remember you are in the presence of
. . . in the present with . . . Jesus.

When we *just live today*, the ordinary moments become gifts.
They become sacred to us. I have a decorative box in my family
room that reads: "Enjoy the little things, for someday, you will
realize they were the BIG things." That reminds me to intentionally
seek out seconds, minutes, or hours of each day and focus on them
as keepsakes for my heart. These keepsake moments are where our
souls find gratitude and where we are filled with the love, joy, peace,
patience, kindness, goodness, gentleness, and *even* self-control that
we receive from the Holy Spirit.

I invite you to slow down with me. Just live in this moment.
Just live today.

Before you hustle out the door in the morning, pause.

Breathe.

Receive the gift of this twenty-four hours. Let's not miss what's
right here, right now. Life is a gift; make it count.

Truth One: Just Live Today

Journaling Experience

1. Find a comfortable place to sit. It might be your favorite
   chair, at the breakfast table, or on your back deck. Maybe
   someplace where you can hear the birds greet the day or
   see your favorite family portrait on the bookshelf in front
   of you. Go to that place and take your Bible and your
   journal with you.
2. Take three long breaths. Close your eyes; envision sitting
   at the feet of Jesus as the sun rises.
3. Have a conversation with the One who knows you intimately, including all your doubts, fears, and frustrations.

Relax in being fully understood and unconditionally loved by Jesus. Ask him, "What is my assignment for today, Lord?"

4. Write down what's in your heart. There's nothing formal or fancy to it. There's no need to worry about grammar or spelling. This isn't about writing something profound or poetic. At first, you might want to jot down your "to-do" list, but God's provision for you to *just live today* is more than the groceries you need, the agenda for the meeting, or the stops you must make on your commute home. It's about sharing your heart with God.

5. What is the Lord saying to you? Keep writing. Perhaps it's just three sentences, or maybe it's a love letter to yourself. Let him guide you as you ponder what it means to *just live today*. Thank Jesus for this quiet time of reflection, this time just between the two of you. Give yourself a hug. Smile. And *just live today*.

Prayer (Speak your own or use this to get you started):

Thank you, Jesus, for the gift of today. Thank you for another day of life. Thank you for all the blessings in my life. For this is the day that you have made, I'm rejoicing and I am glad in it (Ps. 118:24). Today I choose to fix my eyes, not on what is seen, but on what is unseen. For what is seen is temporary, but what is unseen is eternal (2 Cor. 4:18). May your peace rule in my heart all day long as I slow down and keep my focus on you. In your holy name, I pray. Amen.

CHAPTER FOURTEEN

Expect Miracles

Long before he laid down earth's foundations, he had us in mind, had settled on us as the focus of his love, to be made whole and holy by his love. Long, long ago he decided to adopt us into his family through Jesus Christ. (What pleasure he took in planning this!) He wanted us to enter into the celebration of his lavish gift-giving by the hand of his beloved Son. (Eph. 1:4–6 The Message)

FOLLOWING INSTRUCTIONS AND OBEYING RULES is somewhat comforting, because life is often out of control. Throughout this book, you've learned about my personal struggles with feeling unworthy, and the results from believing such lies. As Christian women, we know in our heads that our salvation doesn't depend on what we do, yet many of us try to prove we deserve salvation through good deeds. We help out in the nursery at church, or deliver meals to shut-ins, or make calls for the prayer chain, and show up in the pews regularly with our families, at least in part to show evidence of what we believe—to ourselves and to everyone around us.

The *doing* reassures us that we are who we say we are, and we hope it proves that we are worthy of God's love. While this may not be true for every Christian, many of us often act as though it is the external acts that save us rather than the internal relationship with God.

But what happens when following the rules and doing all the good deeds don't seem to work anymore? When our identity in Christ has not yet taken hold of our lives? When we aren't perfect and we're still trying to gain acceptance and approval from others through our performance? When trying harder just means we continue to fall harder?

We second guess ourselves and question what we believe. We wonder if everything we've ever known to be true is true after all. Feeling lost, we ask ourselves, "Who am I? What do I really believe?" And yet, we don't want to know the answers. So, we keep our doubts stuffed inside and allow walls of fear to build up. Never in a million years would we dare to tell anyone else our secret—that sometimes we question our value to God's kingdom, our worth as women of God, sometimes even God's very existence.

What we fail to realize is that questioning is part of our faith walk and not a severance of our relationship with God. Perhaps some of the effort we put into the external evidence of our faith should be focused on the inward struggles we often have as believers. In God's truth, there is a time and place for both and he expects us to do both—demonstrate Christlike behavior to the outside world as a result of our inner journey with him. Our deeds are an outward expression of his love for us, in us.

Most of my life, I only knew how to *do* religion. I never understood how to *be* a believer in Christ and how to have a relationship with him. I often wondered why I didn't know the Jesus of the Bible like the amazing Christian speakers I so admired, or the friends I interacted with daily.

Why did they seem to "get it" and I didn't?

I accepted Christ as a teenager, but somehow my belief never traveled from my head to my heart. I tried everything, from teaching children's Sunday school and volunteering at church to leading home Bible studies and following annual Bible reading plans. This was the "good church lady" way to live . . . to gain God's favor and earn angel wings. I thought that if I followed the rules perfectly, one day I would *know* Jesus and believe I was worthy to be God's daughter.

In the meantime I looked for my worth in the words and the attention of others. As long as I had my husband's compliments, my friend's approval, or my daughter's responsiveness, my confidence would be boosted just long enough to get me through another day. But on those days when I didn't get the affirmations I needed to fill up my easily-depleted "worthy bucket," my life began to fracture and fall apart.

I believed *in* God, but I did not know how to *believe* God.

The promise of God's unconditional love and grace-filled forgiveness was too much to grasp. I did not believe I was God's beloved daughter, which was the barrier to really believing God.

Have you ever felt like this? Do you wrestle with questions like "How can God love me?" or "After all the ways I've messed up, how can he accept me?" It's so hard for me to remember and fully trust what Emily Ley, creative director of Joy & Simplicity, says: "I will hold myself to a standard of grace, not perfection."

But when we look at the life of Jesus, whom did he minister to? And whom did Jesus ask to join him in ministry? What types of people were given the mission of spreading the gospel? They were all broken, imperfect, unworthy sinners; in fact, in terms of their social worth, they were perceived as some of the least worthy—yet they were the ones chosen to receive his love, forgiveness, and healing.

> Because of the sacrifice of the Messiah, his blood poured out on the altar of the Cross, we're a free people—free of penalties and punishments chalked up by all our misdeeds. And not just barely free, either. Abundantly free! He thought of everything, provided for everything we could possibly need, letting us in on the plans he took such delight in making. He set it all out before us in Christ, a long-range plan in which everything would be brought together and summed up in him, everything in deepest heaven, everything on planet earth. (Eph. 1:7–10 *The Message*)

This is what I hold true now: God will not force himself on us. He waits patiently (giving us free will) for us to turn to him. That's what he did for me. When I finally got desperate enough, I found him and fell in love with Jesus when he unveiled the truth in my heart. I am worthy. I am valued. I am his daughter. I am adored. I am perfect in his sight just the way I am.

It is a miracle I never expected.

Out of brokenness, God restores our messes, our mistakes, our lives.

He takes everything—guilt, shame, pain, rejection, bitterness, our feeling that we aren't forgiven—upon himself and releases us from these burdens. God's grace becomes our peace. The lies we've believed are erased, and truth is revealed. We are free. It is our birthright. Jesus died so that we could live in radical freedom. God weaves it all into a beautiful tapestry: strands of love and perfection in the name of his Son, Jesus. We are a new people. A miracle.

> I, even I, am he who blots out
> > your transgressions, for my own sake,
> > and remembers your sins no more. (Isa. 43:25)

A relationship with Jesus is not difficult. It's one simple truth: a choice.

In desperation, we find him. And, to remain connected to his life-giving comfort, counsel, and peace, we must *choose* to fill our minds with the truth. Living out of our feelings comes naturally—we *are* human—but living by our feelings and emotions can be disastrous. Our feelings are not always true. God's Word, the Bible, is where we find our footing. Best-selling author Lysa TerKeurst says, "Our emotions should be indicators, not dictators."

We are wise to plant our souls in Scripture and root our hope in its promises, never in our feelings. James 1:8 and Philippians 4:8 remind us to keep Jesus at the forefront. Daily, we must choose to believe the Word and embrace the truth that Christ lives in us through the miracle of his powerful Holy Spirit.

> It's in Christ that you, once you heard the truth and
> believed it (this Message of your salvation), found
> yourselves home free—signed, sealed, and delivered
> by the Holy Spirit. This signet from God is the first
> installment on what's coming, a reminder that we'll
> get everything God has planned for us, a praising and
> glorious life. (Eph. 1:13–14 *The Message*)

Because of Christ we see abandoned children being embraced in love, cancer patients being healed, frail bodies being restored to life, addictions being conquered, and broken relationships being renewed. It is wonderful not to have to wait until we get to heaven to witness miracles. Such miracles are to be experienced right here, right now. I experienced that firsthand.

Expecting—even experiencing—miracles doesn't mean that we always get the miracles we want. And we should not take that as a sign that we aren't good Christians or that we are somehow not worthy of a miracle. Sometimes healing doesn't equal a cure. Sometimes the miracle isn't that we live, but how we live through our challenges and our crises and our illnesses. People don't always recover. Everyone dies, and some of us seem to experience an untimely death. In some instances we may be left in circumstances that feel more like a tragedy than a miracle.

Sometimes the miracle we expect and the miracle we receive seem miles apart. Sometimes the best we can manage is to look for and accept and be grateful for the ways Jesus shows up in our lives, even when it isn't what we'd hoped for.

We can live with a sense of expectancy and acceptance and, ultimately, even gratitude, no matter what. That is perhaps the greatest miracle of all.

We know that God causes all things to work together for good to those who love God, to those who are called according to His purpose. (Rom. 8:28 NASB)

I celebrate this mysterious miracle of Jesus, my Savior, the Holy One living inside of me. Because of him, I am God's beloved child, created and claimed just as I am. I am worthy. My body is healthy, and my spirit is whole . . . and I *expect miracles*, because every morning, every new day, God's almighty power is at work in my life. Right here. Right now. Always.

Jesus Christ's entire life is the foundational miracle of our belief. He was born of a virgin (miracle!). He suffered a brutal crucifixion and died. He rose from the grave (miracle!), conquering death so that we have life now and forever (miracle!). We have his gift of the resurrecting Holy Spirit that lives inside us (miracle!) and restores our faith minute by minute and hour by hour.

Jesus' Spirit is alive in us today . . . forgiving, healing, and restoring. Miracles now, miracles every single day. Let's believe. Let's live in the power of the resurrection and *expect miracles*.

Truth Two: Expect Miracles

Journaling Experience

1. Return to your comfortable place to sit with your Bible and journal. Take a few deep breaths. Pray. *Lord, help me to connect with you and experience your presence right now. I expect a miracle to happen in this sacred space.*

2. Write to God. What do you long for? How desperate are you for him? Tell him your doubts or fears. Spill your pain.

3. Meditate over the following five simple truths.
   - I am God's child, his beloved daughter (Gal. 3:26).
   - I am completely forgiven always (1 John 1:9).
   - I am a whole new person with a whole new life (2 Cor. 5:17).
   - I am God's incredible work of art (Eph. 2:10).
   - I am deeply cherished and loved (Rom. 5:8).

4. What are these passages revealing to your heart? Who does God say you are? Dare to see yourself as Jesus sees

you. Take a few minutes and receive his truths. Write them down.

5. Be attentive to God's presence throughout your day. Reflect on who he says you are. Consider making this a personal mantra.

Prayer (Speak your own or use this to get you started):

Thank you, Jesus, for the miracle of your life and resurrection. Thank you for the miracle of my life. I pray that I will not take this day for granted, but, instead, see the ongoing, everyday miracles that surround me. Enlighten the eyes of my heart so that I may know the incomparably great power of Jesus living inside of me (Eph. 1:18–19). Thank you, Lord, for a new perspective. Thank you that I am worthy to be your adored and beloved daughter. In your name I pray. Amen.

CHAPTER FIFTEEN

Speak Truth

For when he spoke, the world began!
It appeared at his command. (Ps. 33:9 NLT)

I SAY SOME FAIRLY FOOLISH THINGS. Hurtful, ugly words to the people I love the most pop right out of my mouth when I'm frustrated or irritable or just tired. Then, I cringe. I wish my mouth had a rewind button.

Maybe that happens to you sometimes, too.

Words are powerful. They can build up or they can tear down. Ephesians 4:29 warns, "Do not let any unwholesome talk come out of your mouths, but only what is helpful for building others up according to their needs, that it may benefit those who listen."

What a great idea, to let nothing but wholesome talk come out of my mouth. But, oh my goodness, is it hard.

It can be especially tough in regard to how we talk to ourselves. Negative self-talk has been my life's struggle. I didn't know I had any other option and accepted it as the way I was. Talking bad about myself *to* myself was just me.

Our kitchens are never clean enough to suit us. Our furnishings never quite stylish enough. Our jobs never quite important enough, compared to the other women in the neighborhood. Our clothes never quite flattering enough. And we never hesitate to tell ourselves how we fail to measure up.

When we go clothes shopping, especially for bathing suits, we stand in front of the full-length mirror and demoralizing words fly out of our mouths. "Ugh! Look at those thighs! How did you ever get in such bad shape? You are an embarrassment. You should be ashamed of how you look. You have no self-control. Why do you keep eating those cookies? Is it really that hard to work out three times a week? How lazy can you be?"

Have you ever spoken to yourself this way?

Consider this: if we were to talk to our friends the way we talk to ourselves, they would not want to stick around. More than likely, we wouldn't be able to hold a job, and our social calendars would be blank.

Or this: Would you talk to a vulnerable child the way you talk to yourself?

Imagine, for a moment, saying some of the things you say to yourself to a child who has just broken a toy or skinned her knee. Imagine telling her how clumsy she is or how stupid he is. Imagine how that child would feel. Imagine the look in his eyes or how quickly tears would roll down her cheeks.

If you wouldn't say something to a hurting child, why on earth would you say it to yourself? Such negativity certainly is not Christ-like and it doesn't help us feel better about our circumstances or ourselves. Christ encourages us to love others as we love ourselves, which means we are supposed to love ourselves. We are his; how can we not love all that is God's?

Have you ever taken a day, or even just an hour, to listen to what you say to yourself? A lot of the time, it's total junk. The "not enough" thoughts bombard the mind: Not enough time. Not enough energy. Not enough money. This litany of self-criticism often includes the most devastating "not enough" of all: "I am not enough."

How much compassion do we give ourselves? Do we shrug it off when things go wrong, or do we continue to beat ourselves up? Do we cut ourselves some slack when we make a mistake, or do we dump blame and shame on our own heads?

What's really a shame is the way we shame ourselves with how human we are. Really.

And as harsh as we are when we're talking to or about ourselves, we do nothing to make it right. We don't regret the words we hurl at ourselves. We don't soothe ourselves afterward. Most of the time, we're quick to take notice of our not-so-kind words to others, and we apologize for our mistakes and make things right with those we have offended. But our self-talk is a different story altogether. We just let that mean language stand. It's time we stop self-berating and start celebrating that we are God's beloved daughters.

∾ ∾ ∾

Recently, after a beach trip with my daughter, I was feeling down. I had anticipated some refreshing mother-daughter bonding time, but the weekend turned out to be more about me nagging her. Fueled by an adolescent hormonal tsunami, my daughter was completely focused on her own physical imperfections—something I recognized all too well from my own personal experiences. In trying hard to convince her that the world did not revolve around her, I said things more harshly than I intended. When it was over, I was disappointed in myself.

What kind of mother talks to her daughter that way? I thought, immediately jumping into the negative self-talk that has been my lifelong pattern. *I've scarred her for life. I'm an awful mother.*

Realizing that I needed to turn my thoughts around and stop beating myself up, I decided that staying home alone wasn't the best idea. I packed up my laptop and books and headed to my favorite coffee shop. While working, I looked up and noticed a man standing in front of my table; he was staring at my Bible and shaking his head. I glanced back at my computer and tried to ignore him. It felt a little freaky.

Finally, because I sensed that he wasn't going to leave until I talked with him, I said a polite hello.

"I can't read the Bible anymore," he said, still shaking his head.

"Why not?" I asked.

"Ever since I've been on pain medication for my back, it's like something is blocking me," he answered, making an up-and-down motion with his hand in front of his body. "I feel numb when I take the medication, so I don't read the Bible anymore."

Quickly I stood up. "May I pray for you?"

He accepted my offer with a warm smile. We bowed our heads, and I prayed. Then, I reached for my Bible, and together we read Psalm 107:19–20: "Then they cried out to the LORD in their trouble, He saved them out of their distresses. He sent His word and healed them, and delivered them from their destructions" (NASB).

I could see hope in this gentleman's weary eyes as he thanked me. "Maybe I can read the Bible again. I just might try today when I get home."

I don't know if the words we read together were ultimately healing for that man or not; that was between him and God. But I know he was in that place so that I would hear those words for myself.

The Word of God will not return void according to Isaiah 55:11, but will accomplish what God desires and achieve a purpose.

After my experience at the coffee shop, I knew I had to set things right with my daughter. I humbled myself, apologized for being too harsh when I spoke to her on our beach trip, and asked for her forgiveness. I also gave myself permission to forgive myself for my parenting mistakes.

The tongue has the power of life and death,
and those who love it will eat its fruit. (Prov. 18:21)

❧ ❧ ❧

Going through cancer and the coma, I learned the power of my thoughts and words. When I woke up in the hospital and could not speak, my thoughts quickly turned from defeat to determination. Backed by the power of the prayers of my family and friends, I insisted that I was going to breathe on my own, get out of the bed, and walk again. I believed that God had not brought me this far to quit. No one was going to stop me. My thoughts became my words, which became my reality.

Do not conform to the pattern of this world, but be transformed by the renewing of your mind. Then you will be able to test and approve what God's will is—his good, pleasing and perfect will. (Rom. 12:2)

This was the Scripture I clung to while undergoing chemotherapy. Little did I know how it would impact the rest of my healing. Words are powerful. All of creation came to be simply through the power of God's Word. "And God said, 'Let there be light,' and there was light" (Gen. 1:3).

God's Word spoke creation into existence. Our words are like the air we breathe. Our words give us life. It's time to believe in the power of our words and the positive impact they can have on us. Speaking the truth out loud has changed my life, my faith, and my relationships with my family and friends. It has helped me let go of all the times in my childhood when I had no voice and learned to think my only real value was in how I looked or how I performed. Now I know that when I speak, Jesus is listening, even if no one else hears. I know this because of my personal relationship with him. Today, I know that when we speak God's Word, we have supernatural power and authority through Christ. And when we speak God's Words to ourselves, we do a better job of encouraging and uplifting with positive self-talk as we face life's challenges.

Speaking God's Word into our own lives or another's life opens their hearts (and ours) to healing. Grammy winner Toby Mac, a Christian hip-hop recording artist, says it best in his song "Speak Life," "Look into the eyes of the brokenhearted; watch them come alive as soon as you speak hope, speak love, speak life."

Just because I spend time with God in my early-morning quiet time or play Christian music in my car does not guarantee that negative thoughts won't pop into my mind. Life hurls struggles at me daily. I must stay on guard and be ready every minute to reject the lies.

To help me turn from a spirit-killing dialogue to life-giving truths, here are five predetermined actions I keep readily available in my back pocket:

1) **Read** the Bible out loud.
2) **Meditate** on a verse.
3) **Pray** with someone.
4) **Write** out my thoughts, and then rewrite them as if I were giving them to my best friend.
5) **Dispute** the lies (negative thoughts) with God's Word. "Is this really what God says, and what God wants me to say?"

Everybody struggles with defeating thoughts; we are not alone in this. The enemy will attack our worth via criticism. We have to stop letting negativity lead us. Instead, take it captive and lead it with the truth. For me, reading and speaking God's inspired truth out loud has become my weapon to cut through the internal negative voices that nag me.

In addition to the five actions I can take, I've also taken the time to memorize five truths, pulled straight from God's Word. Whenever the lies bombard me, I can speak these five truths out loud instead.

1) God will never condemn me. He does not disapprove of me. He does not criticize or blame me. He does not find fault in me (Rom. 8:1–2).
2) God has not given me a spirit of fear and timidity, but of power, love, and self-discipline (2 Tim. 1:7).
3) I am strong, and the Word of God lives in me, and I have overcome the evil one (1 John 2:14).
4) I am in perfect peace because I trust in God as my thoughts stay fixed on him (Isa. 26:3).
5) I have been given authority over all the power of the enemy, and nothing will harm me (Luke 10:19).

For out of the overflow of his heart his mouth speaks.
(Luke 6:45 NIV 1984)

༄ ༄ ༄

One day, while running on a nature trail close to my house, I saw
a woman with two children ahead of me on the trail. She wasn't
old, but she looked worn-out and defeated. As I was about to pass
them, the woman stopped me and asked if there was a playground
somewhere along the path. I told her there wasn't, quickly put my
ear buds back in, and continued running.

But something stopped me. I slowed my pace. Then I turned
and ran back toward the family.

"Excuse me," I said, "but for some reason, I feel like I'm supposed to pray for you. Is there anything you need prayer for today?"

Tears filled the mother's eyes. "We just moved here from
Florida, and we are struggling a little right now. I really need a job."

Stepping off the trail, we all joined hands as I prayed Jeremiah
29:11: "'For I know the plans I have for you,' declares the Lord,
'plans to prosper you and not to harm you, plans to give you hope
and a future.'"

Before we parted ways, I gave her the names of a few churches
in the area. Her face lit up with hope.

I've found that speaking truth into another person's heart
has become the number one strategy for me to overcome my
own negative words toward myself. If I'm having one of those
days when I'm being way too hard on myself, I can cast out the
negativity by turning to another and speaking a word of healing
or love into them.

Because this strategy has become so powerful for me, I have
deliberately written out specific verses on three-by-five notecards

to keep with me. When I find my daughter is going through a hard time (what teen doesn't?), I look up specific Scriptures for her situation and make two cards, one for her and one for myself. Then in the morning before school or in the evening before bed, I read the Scripture to her and remind her that I'm praying it over her.

The lyrics by Hawk Nelson in their song "Words" is the prayer of my heart and the hope for my mouth. "Let my words be life / Let my words be truth / I don't wanna say a word / Unless it points the world back to You."

If I'm ever tempted to think that words aren't all that important, all I need to do to remind myself otherwise is look to the Gospel according to John. "In the beginning was the Word, and the Word was with God, and the Word was God. . . . The Word became flesh and made his dwelling among us" (1:1, 14a).

That's so deep I'm not always sure exactly what to make of it. But I get this much: Jesus is the Word made flesh, the revelation of God's Word.

God used the power of words to speak the world into being. The Word came to us in the form of Jesus Christ. These two things alone tell me that as a child of God, I must never underestimate the power of my words.

Truth Three: Speak Truth

Journaling Experience

1. Go to your cozy quiet place where you can be alone with God, your Bible, and your journal. Take a few long breaths.
2. Open up your Bible and read Philippians 4:4–7. Write it down in your journal.

3. Now read it aloud several times.
4. Personalize the passage and *speak truth* into yourself: "Linda, rejoice in the Lord always." Then, read aloud the passage in affirmation: "I will rejoice in the Lord always. I will say it again, rejoice." Finally, use the Scripture as a prayer: "Thank you, Lord, that I can rejoice in you always. . . . I receive your peace that transcends all understanding. Thank you, Jesus, for guarding my mind and filling my heart with your love."
5. As this discipline becomes more natural to you, it will be comforting, and it will transfer into how you speak truth to yourself and others. Life-giving words uplift and change lives. Jesus gives you the words, and the Holy Spirit empowers you. *Speak truth.*

Prayer (Speak your own or use this to get you started):

Thank you, heavenly Father, for your holy Word that has been preserved for more than three thousand years. Your Words are a sacred blessing in my life. I cannot imagine a day without them. May I use my mouth to speak truth into my life and into the lives of everyone I encounter today. I stand confident that, when I speak your living Word, it will do a great work, because it cannot return to you void (Isa. 55:11). In Jesus' name I pray and give thanks.
Amen.

CHAPTER SIXTEEN

Use Your Gifts

I tell you the truth, anyone who has faith in me will do what I have been doing. He will do even greater things than these, because I am going to the Father. And I will do whatever you ask in my name, so that the Son may bring glory to the Father. You may ask me for anything in my name, and I will do it. (John 14:12–14 NIV 1984)

DAY IN AND DAY OUT, we go through the motions. Car pool, work routines, cleaning, grocery shopping, cooking, laundry, helping kids with homework, TV, even scheduling time with friends, our date nights with our spouses. It's all monotony. Ordinary routines sometimes become dreadful days.

Emptiness and, over time, even resentment can set in over the lack of excitement or meaning in our lives. And we might even start to feel guilty over these feelings.

We find ourselves saying, "I should appreciate my life. I should be grateful." Then, we give ourselves a pep talk . . . only to fall back into the same old routine of monotony, boredom, and, finally, that sense of emptiness.

It's easy to throw up our hands and wonder if this is all there is, if life has any purpose. Deep down, we might secretly be carrying around a sense of insignificance. The world we live in screams that our purpose, worth, and importance are found in fame and fortune. And here we are, buried in boredom and meaninglessness.

At some point, usually in the middle of our life, we hit that insistent, questioning state of demanding to know what on earth we are here for. We want to know if there is some purpose to life besides pouring cereal, paying bills, cleaning house, going to work, and coming home.

> It's in Christ that we find out who we are and what we
> are living for. Long before we first heard of Christ and
> got our hopes up, he had his eye on us, had designs on
> us for glorious living, part of the overall purpose he is
> working out in everything and everyone. (Eph. 1:11–12
> *The Message*)

Everyone these days seems to be asking about purpose and meaning in life. That says a lot about the hollowness of our lives in this day and time, I think. Everyone is writing and reading books about how to find meaning—how to find our purpose.

As Christians, we might examine what the Bible has to say about our spiritual gifts. Yes, we all have natural talents. We can sing, or we can garden, or we are brilliant in math or science. But the gifts I'm talking about here are entirely different from our God-given talents.

We might turn to the Bible and begin to ask ourselves, "Which gifts have I been given?" We might even become fixated on labeling ourselves with the exact gifts that suit us best. Hospitality? Leadership? Mercy? Teaching? and so on. In 1 Corinthians 12:4–11, Paul teaches us that we have different kinds of gifts, but they all come from the same Spirit. Whether it's the gift of wisdom, knowledge, faith, healing, prophecy, or speaking or interpreting tongues, we need to use them while we are living on earth, because they will no longer be needed in eternity—in eternity, everything will be complete. Gifts are to edify the believer in order to build up the church here in this life.

Our hope is to nail down exactly what our gifts are, so that we will know our purpose in life.

The snare here is that we can get trapped into focusing inward, thinking it's all about us. Christine Caine, the founder of the A21 Campaign, a non-profit that combats human trafficking, spoke at my church recently. What she said blew my mind and probably ruffled a few Christian feathers as well.

Christine said that when she started attending church more than twenty-five years ago, she went to get help. Her life was a mess; she had suffered a childhood of sexual abuse. With the help of the church she found the healing only God could provide. What a gift! But then, she said, a time came when she had received all the help she needed from the church. Now it was time for her to stop taking and start giving.

I could feel God stretching my spirit as I contemplated her words. "Stop taking and start giving."

It's easy to go to church and expect it to fill me up—teach me, serve me, and even stroke my ego just a little because I volunteer every other week. But if we are not careful, we can slip into seeking primarily our own fulfillment and satisfaction—a seeking which serves not the body of Christ, but self.

I admit, I used to spend a lot of time asking myself, "What's going to work best for me?" and "What do I enjoy doing most?" Serving Jesus was wrapped up in self-seeking motives. And this approach ultimately kept me in the mode of *doing* religion instead of using the gifts God bestowed on me to *be* a gift in the kingdom.

Our human desire can so easily become the urge to fit all the pieces of our Christian experience together perfectly so that they align with *our* ambitions, *our* goals, and *our* dreams.

While I absolutely agree with having ambitions, goals, and dreams, it's finally becoming clear to me that those things work well in my life only when they are grounded in the desire and determination to serve Jesus.

When people volunteer at my church, they go through an informational training meeting to learn about the different volunteer opportunities. Many years ago when I attended the meeting, I went into it thinking I was going to sign up for what sounded the most fun and what would benefit me. But when it was time to choose what team I would serve on, my heart sent me in a completely different direction. It was not something I really desired to do. I wrestled with myself for a little while before making a decision, but I knew God was leading me to this team—the prayer team.

In those days, I did not like to pray out loud and I did not feel comfortable praying with others. I remember thinking prayer really was not my thing.

So why in the world would I feel led to sign up for this role in my church? Well, because God had a gift waiting for me. And it was not just any ordinary gift; it was a sacred one, a gift that I now cherish every day of my life.

When we think of gifts, they are usually things we are happy to receive. Maybe we have been patiently waiting for that special gift for some time—a raise or a promotion at work, an engagement ring, a pregnancy, a new car. So when I joined the prayer team, it didn't appear to me to be a gift at all. Instead of gaining something, it felt like I was losing something. Which actually was very true. I was losing myself.

> Then Jesus said to his disciples, "If any of you wants to
> be my follower, you must turn from your selfish ways,
> take up your cross, and follow me." (Matt. 16:24 NLT)

Gifts from God come in many different forms, such as relationships, success, or a good health report. We love to receive gifts, especially if they appear to immediately benefit us. But I dare to say that the best gifts from God are the ones that stretch you, challenge you, and move you out of your comfort zone. Gifts that might not seem like gifts at first, the gifts that have the potential to build our character. For example, when you want to cut off someone in traffic but you decide to slow down instead and let him or her in front of you. Or when you want to gossip about someone because they hurt you badly, but instead you choose to pray blessings for them.

> And what do you benefit if you gain the whole world
> but lose your own soul? (Mark 8:36 NLT)

How can we make sure we are using our gifts the way God intends? Here are five markers we can use to monitor the way we're using our gifts.

1. Identify our gifts not by what sounds fun, but by praying for guidance. Many churches use spiritual gift assessments these days; some are even available online. We should go into this seeking process with an open heart

and mind, focused on finding ways to be of service and not ways to satisfy ourselves.

2. Give in ways that don't benefit us.
3. Give anonymously. Whether it is financial gifts or gifts of service, if we find that we rarely give unless the gift is acknowledged, we may find that we're giving with strings attached.
4. Give sacrificially.
5. Watch for the ways your gifts multiply. When given away, our gifts multiply in our own lives and in the lives of those who receive them.

∿ ∿ ∿

We are called to be the body of Christ, "the fullness of him who fills everything in every way" (Eph. 1:23). God lives through us. What we do, what we speak, and how we live continues to fill his purpose for our lives.

This reminds me of a Christian woman who had enrolled her child in a private school that taught evolution. The school was open to discuss all beliefs. They studied various religions, including Christianity. Students shared their personal beliefs in conversations in the classroom, which tended to cause a bit of controversy between students.

When her child spoke up to the teacher and requested not to participate in visiting the different religious organizations because it made her uncomfortable, the teacher mocked her in front of her classmates. "Don't be ignorant. It's not like they are going to convert you," the teacher said.

As you can imagine, her child was upset by what happened. The child's mother could have approached this situation out of anger. Instead she used her gifts of wisdom and faith. She took her child's hand and said, "Sweetie, let's pray for your teacher to come to know Jesus. Maybe instead of being mad at her, we can simply love her just the way she is. After all, that's what Jesus does for us every single day."

What a beautiful gift from God, for this mother to demonstrate to her daughter what it is to allow Jesus to live through them.

As believers, we are faced with this challenge almost every minute of our lives. Are we going to live by our flesh, our desires, and our feelings, or are we going to use the gifts of God living inside of us?

> Now God has us where he wants us, with all the time in this world and the next to shower grace and kindness upon us in Christ Jesus. Saving is all his idea, and all his work. All we do is trust him enough to let him do it. It's God's gift from start to finish! We don't play the major role. If we did, we'd probably go around bragging that we'd done the whole thing! No, we neither make nor save ourselves. God does both the making and saving. He creates each of us by Christ Jesus to join him in the work he does, the good work he has gotten ready for us to do, work we had better be doing. (Eph. 2:7–10 *The Message*)

"It's God's gift." The simple discipline of thanking God and trusting him will allow us to live in the gift of his endless presence. Use the gift of his holy indwelling love to join God in his good work, and find your purpose.

Remember, when we use our gifts, we don't become worthy of a miracle—we become part of the miracle. Using our gifts multiplies the miracles in the world.

When you do this, the gift will return to you as joy.

Truth Four: Use Your Gifts

Journaling Experience

1. As you get comfortable with your Bible and journal, take a few deep breaths. Pray this simple prayer: *Thank you, God. I trust you, God.* You might even meditate on this prayer for a few minutes.

2. Find a Scripture that spoke to you in this chapter.

3. Look up the verse in different translations to begin exploring the meaning more deeply. Bible Gateway online is a great tool, because it will allow you the option to view multiple translations at the same time. Choose the translation that speaks most clearly to you. Read it out loud. Journal about why it speaks to you. Then choose the translation that does not speak to you. Read it out loud. Journal about what in this translation may be making you uncomfortable or uneasy. Ask yourself if there is a place for you to grow—in other words, is there a gift for you—by embracing the translation that does not speak to you.

4. What is the Lord saying to you about this passage? Write a letter to God thanking him for the gift of his Spirit within you that is guiding you.

5. Sitting with gratitude and an open heart, think about how you will begin to intentionally use the gifts God has given you.

Prayer (Speak your own or use this to get you started):

Thank you, God, for the gift of your Spirit dwelling inside me (1 Cor. 3:16). Thank you, Lord, that I no longer have to wonder what on earth I am here for, but instead know that I live to reflect your love. I pray I will live my life in honor and service to you, Jesus. May I always be a blessing to others. In your name I pray. Amen.

CHAPTER SEVENTEEN

Start Now!

Then Jesus went to work on his disciples. "Anyone who intends to come with me has to let me lead. You're not in the driver's seat; I am. Don't run from suffering; embrace it. Follow me and I'll show you how. Self-help is no help at all. Self-sacrifice is the way, my way, to finding yourself, your true self. What kind of deal is it to get everything you want but lose yourself? What could you ever trade your soul for?" (Matt. 16:24–26 The Message)

GOD DOESN'T SET AN ALARM CLOCK. He doesn't text you if you don't return his call. Jesus waits. He waits patiently. I like to say he is a gentleman because he does not force himself on you.

A friend of mine once said she imagines Jesus waiting on her at the kitchen table when she wakes up in the morning. Some days she's guilty of rushing through her morning and not even giving him a hello or a thank you for stopping by. Other days on her way to bed she's reminded that he has been waiting for her all day, patiently hoping to be noticed.

One day she thought, *What if that were my husband or children sitting there? Of course, I would talk with them. I would stop and*

give them a hug or kiss and tell them how much I love them. I would
make sure I took time to connect with them. How much more does
Jesus deserve that from me?

After that revelation, she began to schedule an appointment at 5:00 A.M. every morning to meet with Jesus.

I can promise you that I never go twenty-hour hours without speaking to my spouse (unless I'm doing the "silent treatment" dance after an argument, which I'm embarrassed to admit sometimes happens). So why would I go an entire day without talking to God?

Developing a personal relationship with Jesus takes intention, consistency, and a hunger to spend time alone with him.

Do you have a predetermined plan for building intimacy with God? If not, it's time to stop procrastinating and start now.

∿ ∿ ∿

I never procrastinate when it's time to do something I really want to do. I don't procrastinate when there's a pint of Ben and Jerry's in my freezer—I can hardly wait to open that carton, grab my spoon, and dig in. I don't procrastinate when there's a book I've been dying to read—I just start. The sooner, the better.

But when it comes to doing the things that are going to have the biggest and best and most significant payoffs, what do I do? I put them off.

Starting that new exercise routine? Next week will be soon enough. Cleaning out the garage? Maybe later.

For some reason that's hard for me to get a handle on. Doing the things that are really going to be good for me is as hard as eating my vegetables. I know that, in the end, I'm going to be glad I ate those vegetables. They even taste good! But I just keep thinking,

No, I'll get around to that spinach salad tomorrow for lunch. Tonight, I think I'll pop that frozen pizza in the oven instead.

Like frozen pizza is all that grand?

Maybe I'm just emotionally, spiritually, or physically lazy. (Or maybe that's the critical voice I try to ignore, worming its way into my head again when I'm not paying much attention.)

Or maybe it's that deeply buried part of me that still—still!—doesn't believe I'm worthy of doing the thing that's going to really be good for me. The thing that's going to keep me fit and healthy, keep my mind sharp, enhance my friendships, make my home comfortable and inviting—the good stuff that fills me up.

I don't know what it is in me that makes it so easy to do the wrong thing and not do the right thing. But I know I'm not alone. The apostle Paul, in his letter to the Romans, said, "I don't really understand myself, for I want to do what is right, but I don't do it. Instead, I do what I hate" (7:15 NLT).

Maybe you find yourself doing the same thing.

Here's what I learned the hard way about procrastination: we never know when it's going to be too late to start doing what we know is right.

Maybe you've seen the cute line on Facebook or elsewhere that says: Life is uncertain. Eat dessert first.

Life is uncertain. And the dessert is not what we think it is. The dessert isn't that carton of Ben and Jerry's. Dessert is living the JESUS life.

So let's eat dessert first. Let's start now!

∽ ∽ ∽

What does it mean to start now?

It means to start spending time with Jesus. Not randomly. Not from time to time. Every day. Consistently. By reading the Bible, praying, and journaling conversations with him. It means finding the sacred space where we can get alone with Jesus and nurture this relationship, the most precious relationship in our lives.

It means choosing the Jesus way in our actions, our words, and our relationships.

It means living in this very moment fully aware that we are precious children of God—and so is everyone else in our lives. Then treating ourselves and others as if we know this deep in our souls.

It means being a gift in the lives of others.

It means knowing we'll stumble around and get it wrong and have to pick ourselves up, brush the gravel off our skinned knees, and start over again without beating ourselves up or belittling ourselves.

❧ ❧ ❧

Pastor Steven Furtick, of Elevation Church, once said, "Often in isolation is where God brings revelation."

Learning how to be in relationship with Jesus takes time. We understand his character through studying the Bible, talking with others about their experiences with him, and stepping out of our comfort zone to be his hands and feet. Jesus cares, counsels, guides, and heals. He's tender. He's compassionate. He's generous. He's humble. And the more time we spend with him, the more we become like him. Our character grows.

I talk with him just like I am talking with a best friend. Often I pray in silence, but sometimes I talk out loud. And other times I write down the words I'm speaking to him. Jesus knows *everything* about me, so our conversations come easily. All we have to do is start. Now.

Writing this book is an example of how hard it can be to start on the things that will ultimately serve the greatest good in our lives. I've been called to write this book for years. I put it off. I made false starts. I decided it was a foolish goal for me to even consider. Yet God created this hunger in me to share with the world how I've struggled with feelings of unworthiness my entire life. Maybe, through me, others can understand how worthy we all are as his beloved children. Writing this book was not easy, but the hardest part was just starting.

For when I am weak, then I am strong. (2 Cor. 12:10)

What are the things you struggle with? The things you put off? The things you know will transform your life, but you procrastinate because it's easier to just eat the Ben and Jerry's?

You know what your struggles are, but I want to encourage you to get them out of your head—where, if you're anything like me, they can make you crazy—and into some concrete form. *Then* you can give those struggles to God. *Then* you'll be prepared to tackle them.

Then you can start to realize just how worthy you are in God's eyes to accept the miracles he has in mind for you.

∾ ∾ ∾

On my fortieth birthday, exactly five years after I was in a coma, I signed with my publisher to write this book.

Even as I signed the contract, I wasn't sure I was worthy of telling this story, of speaking into your life about your worthiness and the miracles God is already working for you.

But I knew that, even with all my doubts and fears, God was proving to me all over again that I was worthy by sending a publisher to help me share my story with you.

As I've spent many hours at my laptop reliving my life—God's story—typing one word at a time with tears of heartache and joy, I've come to accept that life is a beautiful struggle. I'm not going to lie. Some days I cave in to my weaknesses and just get by. But then there are those days when I embrace life with every breath.

I *just live today*. I *expect miracles*. I *speak truth*. I *use my gifts*.

As a Christian Life Coach, I encourage you and challenge you to begin an intimate relationship with Jesus. Life's too short to let another second go by without him.

Start now!

Truth Five: Start Now!

Journaling Experience

1. Bring a glass of water and your Bible to a quiet place. Read John 4:13–14: "Jesus answered, 'Everyone who drinks of this water will be thirsty again, but whoever drinks the water I give them will never thirst. Indeed, the water I give them will become in them a spring of water welling up to eternal life.'"

2. Look closely at the JESUS steps in previous chapters of this book. Pray for guidance on how to live each of those steps in a way that God has designed just for you. Write down what you hear as a result of listening to how God responds.

3. Write about your commitment to taking those steps. Think of this journaling as a direct communication with

Jesus. Tell him where you've messed up in the past and how you want to commit to doing things differently as you go forward. Pray and ask him to show up in your day and keep you on track.

4. Pray for God to send someone you can be accountable to for your new life of seeking to be in relationship with Jesus. It may be a Christian coach. It may be a friend who understands your longing to be in active daily relationship with Jesus and is making the same choice. Then make an intentional choice to check in regularly with that person about how you are carrying out your commitments to live the JESUS way as you go forward.

5. Begin your personal relationship with Jesus today. Share your commitments with Jesus through journaling, prayer, and ongoing conversation with him. Don't wait until tomorrow, either. *Start now!*

Prayer (Speak your own or use this to get you started):

Thank you, Jesus, that through my struggles your strength wins. I do not dread or fear my day or my life. I can do all things because you have already overcome the world. You have not given me a spirit of fear and timidity, but a spirit of power, love, and self-discipline (2 Tim. 1:7). I will not let hardships determine my steps but will start with your holy Word that will faithfully direct me. I choose right now to start fully relying on you. In your name I pray. Amen.

Conclusion

For God so loved the world that he gave his one and only Son, that whoever believes in him shall not perish but have eternal life. For God did not send his Son into the world to condemn the world, but to save the world through him. (John 3:16–17)

I DON'T KNOW HOW PERSONAL separation from God seems to show up in your life. I don't know what self-defeating behaviors or beliefs keep you from living in direct relationship with Jesus every day.

Maybe it's perfectionism. Maybe it's feelings of being unworthy, heaping criticism on your own shoulders. Maybe it's just the everyday busyness of life that starts a spiral into craziness and separation. Whatever it is, you can stop it. Today. Right now. And when things spiral out of control again tomorrow or later this afternoon, you can do it again.

I seriously doubt if you're going to get it right every day. I don't. I don't know anyone who does.

I just know people who pick themselves up and take the time to reconnect with God and keep moving forward.

We make progress. That's all. We don't get to be perfect, and we don't have to be perfect. We just keep trying to live the JESUS way. We can:

- Just live today.
- Expect miracles.
- Speak truth.
- Use your gifts.
- Start now!

You don't even have to remember or do all these things every day. If you take away one of these ideas and incorporate it into your daily practice of the presence of God, your life will be better. Just one of these steps will help you make progress in overcoming your personal obstacles to being in relationship with Jesus. If you latch onto one of these steps when life throws you for a loop and you end up on your knees—literally or figuratively—your identity as a child of God will begin to take on new life. You will begin to believe you are worthy of love and miracles, worthy of the gifts he has especially for you.

The JESUS way isn't something for you to add to your to-do list. It isn't one more way for you to measure yourself and decide if you come up short. It's just an example of what has worked for me—and a reminder that there's a pathway for you, as well.

Because wherever you are on your faith journey, you are worthy.

Recognize the miracles in your life today. Feel the love of Jesus surrounding you today. Accept your hug from Jesus. Put your arms around yourself and give yourself a squeeze. And if you believe nothing else, believe this: God loves you exactly where you are today. Nothing will change that. God's love is infinite, and it is yours.

And, yes, that is a miracle.